DIVINATION WITH THE TAROT

A Beginner's Guide to Tarot Reading

MONIQUE JOINER SIEDLAK

Disclaimer Notice

Please note the information contained within this document is for educational and entertainment purposes only. All effort has been executed to present accurate, up to date, reliable, complete information. No warranties of any kind are declared or implied. Readers acknowledge that the author is not engaged in the rendering of legal, financial, medical or professional advice. The content within this book has been derived from various sources. Please consult a licensed professional before attempting any techniques outlined in this book.

By reading this document, the reader agrees that under no circumstances is the author responsible for any losses, direct or indirect, that are incurred as a result of the use of the information contained within this document, including, but not limited to, errors, omissions, or inaccuracies.

Divination with the Tarot: A Beginner's Guide to Tarot Reading © Copyright 2022 by Monique Joiner Siedlak

All rights reserved

The content contained within this book may not be reproduced, duplicated or transmitted without direct written permission from the author or the publisher.

Legal Notice

This book is copyright protected. It is only for personal use. You cannot amend, distribute, sell, use, quote or paraphrase any part, or the content within this book, without the consent of the author or publisher.

ISBN: 978-1-956319-68-2 (Paperback)

ISBN: 978-1-956319-69-9 (Hardcover)

ISBN: 978-1-956319-67-5 (eBook)

Cover Design by MJS

Cover Image by depositphotos.com/Amaviael

Oshun Publications

701 Market Street Suite 110-6035

Saint Augustine, FL 32095

www.oshunpublications.com

Books in the Series

Divination Magic for Beginners

Divination with Runes: A Beginner's Guide to Rune Casting

Divination with Diloggún: A Beginner's Guide to Diloggún and Obi

Divination with Osteomancy: A Beginner's Guide to Throwing the Bones

Contents

Introduction	xi
1. Card Reading Basics	1
2. Major Arcana	7
3. Minor Arcana	35
4. The One and Two Card Spreads	97
5. Three Card Spread	101
6. Five Card Spread	105
7. More Spreads	109
8. Choosing Your Deck	119
9. Care for Your Cards	121
Conclusion	125
References	127
About the Author	129
More Books by Monique	131

Introduction

Tarot is an ancient divination tool used across cultures to gain insight into all aspects of life and spiritual growth. It deals with the subconscious—that part of our mind that is inaccessible to us but affects all our actions and feelings—and lets us tap into it. Tarot may as well be seen as a road map to our subconscious, offering us an insight into our feelings and thoughts through card readings.

We do a tarot reading by shuffling and cutting our deck and then drawing one or more cards—depending on our spread—and afterward, we search for meaning in those we have chosen. The cards we picked may seem like a random choice, but what is randomness? When something occurs randomly, that event is actually one of all the probable outcomes that were likely to happen. Therefore, it is not really a random event but a chance occurrence. We may say that it was meant to happen or—when it comes to Tarot—that they meant it for us to pick those cards.

Chance is not the only thing that plays a part in tarot readings. What makes reading possible is our conscious way of shuffling the cards in a specific way, cutting them at a certain

Introduction

point, and teaching ourselves how to interpret them beforehand. What occurs by chance—but only after having done our conscious actions—is picking our cards. We could say that tarot reading involves both our conscious and subconscious.

Tarot is a combination of personal perceptions and universal interpretations. We, as human beings, have every day needs and experiences, and the cards reflect them accordingly. How we read the cards is based on intuition and universal meanings. The cards represent patterns of thoughts and emotions, and we use intuition to interpret them following our needs. They are used as a guide for finding solutions to problems that might arise in the future and for gaining wisdom and insight into our current situations.

The origins of the Tarot are mysterious. Cards similar to those we use today for readings first appeared in the late 14th century in Italy and France. In the beginning, Tarot was a card game, and the most popular sets were bought by wealthy families. The printing press did not exist yet, and it cost a fortune to commission card sets since they were all hand-painted.

It was in the late 1700s that tarot cards began to be used as a divination tool. Frenchman Jean-Baptiste Alliette published the first guide to tarot card reading alongside his own deck. In his guide, each card had a meaning. He included beliefs about the four elements—earth, air, water, and fire—and astronomy. He became the first professional tarot reader.

In 1909, Arthur Edward Waite released the famous Rider-Waite deck, illustrated by Pamela Colman Smith. They also included a guide explaining the meaning of each card. When placed together, the illustrations on the cards tell a story.

There are many tarot decks nowadays. The one that is considered traditional, which is also the most popular one, is the

Introduction

Rider-Waite deck. Each deck we use today is based on the Venetian Tarot, consisting of 78 cards. The cards are divided into two groups—the Major Arcana and the Minor Arcana.

The pictures depicted in the Major Arcana cards represent a variety of characters and the journey of our lives. The Minor Arcana cards are divided into four suits—Cups, Wands, Pentacles, and Swords. Each has ten numbered cards (Ace to 10) and four court cards—Page, Knight, Queen, and King.

ONE

Card Reading Basics

It may seem daunting when entering the world of tarot reading. There are many things to read, understand, and learn —but in reality, what we need most is to build a deep connection with our deck. Take a moment each day to study your cards. What does the illustration tell you? What do you feel when you look at the card?

It is crucial to keep an open mind and trust your intuition. Each card has an energy ready to communicate with you—try to embrace it. Before your first reading, let yourself connect with your cards. Study them and try to understand what they depict. Their meaning is in their illustration.

Trust that you already know the meanings of each card. As we have discussed before, they represent patterns of feelings and thoughts that each of us experiences in life. You will only need help to articulate what you see in each card. We'll discuss each of their meanings in the following chapters to aid you, but before that, try to establish a connection with your deck.

When you do your first reading, choose a place with positive energy. Your surroundings must let you focus on what you want to ask your cards. Find a quiet, positive place where you can let your thoughts focus only on what you want to discuss with your deck.

Where you do your reading is not the only one that matters—your headspace is also important. Don't let your thoughts wander to all the issues and problems that may fill your mind at that moment. You might meditate for a bit before you do your reading. Clearing your mind is an essential aspect before delving into a reading.

When you are ready to do your first reading, remember one of the most important things about Tarot that is often misunderstood—the cards cannot tell you what will happen, but what might happen. They will offer guidance on how to deal with the issues that might arise or the problems you are going through while you're reading. Tarot cards can tell you about the past and the present, and when it comes to the future, they can only show you a possibility—our future is not set in stone. It changes with every decision we make and every action we take.

Before doing your first reading, take some time to cleanse your cards. Getting your first tarot deck holds the energy of all who have handled it before you. Each of us carries some energy, and your deck should only connect to yours. By cleansing, you remove all the residual energy left within them and ensure your reading's accuracy, clarity, and connection with the cards. We will thoroughly discuss the cleansing of tarot cards in the last chapter. For now, consider an easy way to do it that will also help you develop a connection with your deck.

For your new tarot deck, cleanse your cards by sorting and shuffling them. By doing this, you cleanse your deck and form and strengthen your connection with it. Lay your cards out, starting with the Major Arcana, then the Minor Arcana. Take some time to look at their imagery and try to understand what the illustrations want to portray, what story they depict, and what their hidden symbols are. When you're done, randomly mix all of your cards and shuffle them.

Now that you've cleansed the deck, it is time to do your reading and ask your cards a question. Think about broader questions that will not limit the answers the cards will give you.

Here are a few examples of questions you can ask your deck.

- Why am I feeling… about…?
- What outcome is most likely if I…?
- What do I need to know about…?
- What is the best step for me to take now?
- What should I do about…?
- How can I understand…?
- What should I take into consideration when/if…?
- What obstacle do I need to overcome to…?
- Am I headed in the right direction?
- What should I focus on regarding…?
- What do I need to do to…?
- How can I improve my…?
- What is currently blocking me from…?
- What mistakes am I making?
- What are their feelings for me?

- What can I do to strengthen my relationship with…?
- What do I need to do to feel stronger/happier/etc.?
- What are my strengths/weaknesses when it comes to…?

Remember not to ask two or more questions simultaneously, such as "Why am I feeling like this and what should I do if I decide to…?" Ask only a single question when addressing your tarot deck. Some answers may be harder to understand if the question is not clear.

You may also choose not to ask questions. Perhaps you would like a simple outlook on your life when you're asking—the cards can offer you that.

For your first reading, consider a simple one-card spread. Each tarot card holds significant meaning and is rich in symbolism. By doing a few one-card readings, you familiarize yourself more easily with your deck and slowly learn their meanings by knowing what to look for in a card. Don't feel discouraged at first if you cannot see what the cards want to tell you yet. Learning Tarot is a long but beautiful process of getting to know the deck, connecting with it, improving your intuition, and gradually gaining more insight into your life.

When you are ready with your question, focus on it and shuffle your cards. Shuffling allows us to meditate on what we want to ask our cards, clear our minds, and center ourselves and our energy to connect with our deck.

Since tarot card reading is based on intuition, shuffle the cards in the way you feel is right. You can do the overhand shuffle by holding your deck in one hand and using the other to mix the cards. You can cut the deck—divide it into two or more piles—and place them together again; repeat this process a few times. You can spread them all facedown, mix them, and then collect them back in a single pile.

Divination with the Tarot

Make sure you divide your deck when you're using reversals—we'll discuss the reversed meanings of the cards in the following two chapters. You flip one pile, so the cards in that pile are reversed. When you use reversals, the card's meaning changes depending on its position—it may show up in a spread, either upright or reversed.

After shuffling, it is time to pull your cards. You can do this in several ways—let your intuition guide you and choose what feels right to you.

You can pull a card by dividing the deck into two piles and picking the card from the top. Another way to do it is by spreading them all out and selecting the one your eye is drawn to. You can also place your deck down, weaken your hold on it, and choose a card from where a gap forms.

Depending on your spread, you can pick a card or several cards. As we've discussed earlier, a single card reading is the easiest to do in the beginning. When you feel ready, you can try to do three-card readings. Tarot spreads that use three or more cards offer more insight into your questions and a more in-depth answer than a single card reading. But they may be more complicated when you have just delved into the world of Tarot.

After you pick your card, lay it face down in your spread, and flip it over. If you decide to use reversals, always flip your cards horizontally so that you do not change the card's original orientation.

Look at your card and try to use your intuition to understand its meaning. What does the illustration represent? What are the colors and symbols depicted in the card? How does it relate to you and your question? How does the card make you feel? Don't worry if you cannot clearly see the meaning yet. You don't have to know everything in the beginning—start your journey by studying the cards' meanings in the following two chapters. You will gradually learn as you do more readings.

TWO

Major Arcana

THE MAJOR ARCANA CARDS REPRESENT SITUATIONS THAT WE all go through during our lives. They deal with the bigger picture of our lives—each card aims to help you when you need perspective and guidance. The cards also focus on your life's long-term direction. They deal with universal human experiences and needs and represent a journey through life and all the issues accompanying it.

The Major Arcana consists of 21 numbered cards and a single one that is unnumbered—the Fool. The Fool is one character of these cards that plays an important role in the story that they portray—he is the one who undertakes the journey depicted in the illustrations of each card.

When doing a reading, the appearance of a high number of Major Arcana cards means it is time to look at your life and reflect on its course. A single Major Arcana card holds a significant meaning that will influence the entire reading.

0 - The Fool

The Fool represents a new beginning or a new opportunity, as well as courage, potential, curiosity, and spontaneity; it may also mean an end to something in your life. The card indicates new experiences and personal growth.

As we've said before, The Fool is the one who undergoes the journey of life depicted in the Major Arcana. He is not a foolish character, as we may think. Still, an innocent youth is taking his first steps into the world joyfully and excitedly, desiring great things but unaware of the many dangers he may encounter in his journey.

Just like the Fool, you are about to embark on a new journey that you know nothing about, and this card warns you about the choices you must carefully make. Critical decisions lie ahead, and you must examine your options and make the best decisions. It is a time of great opportunities and potential, but you must be careful with the risks you might take.

The Fool encourages you to leave behind any fear or worry you might have. He inspires curiosity and open-mindedness and is excited about a new beginning. Your life will change, but it will be for the best. Take a chance and embark on your new journey.

Reversed

When the Fool shows up reversed in your reading, the card warns you about your lack of carefulness. Like the Fool, you find yourself at the edge of a cliff, a dangerous position—you did not think about the repercussions of your actions. You're acting recklessly, and you're taking too many risks. You're spontaneous, but the consequences of the actions that you're taking can significantly affect you.

Don't be fooled by things that seem too good to be true—in the card, the Fool should be more aware of his surroundings, just like you should be of any risks you take and how they might affect your life.

The Fool may also show you are ready for a change, but it is not yet the time for it. You feel held back by something and are not prepared to move forward. You worry about what will happen and are not yet willing to take a chance. The card has your back—as long as you carefully examine your options, set aside your worries, and bring about the change.

1 - The Magician

The Magician card represents strong willpower. The connection between the spiritual and physical realms can also be seen as a connection between the mind and the world—they are only a reflection of each other. What the mind wants, the mind can bring to life into the world. He takes the potential of the Fool and, with the help of the elements of the suits and the connection that he has with both the spiritual and the physical realm, he brings out his potential.

When the Magician shows up in your reading, it is time to leave behind your hesitation and believe in your potential. The card offers the resources you need to bring forth any change you wish for. You have the help of all four elements. The earth is associated with grounding and foundation, water represents intuition and emotion, the air is correlated with intellect, and fire represents inner strength or willpower. The energy of the Magician's connection with the spiritual and physical realm.

Holding back would only mean the loss of a great opportunity —be it a new job, a new relationship, a new project, or something else. The card indicates your determination and strength of will, and you are called to take action and turn your goals and ideas into reality. Welcome the power that the Magician offers you and brings about good changes in your life.

Reversed

When the Magician card shows up reversed in your reading, it might mean that it is time for a change. You are currently considering it but are not taking action because you're not yet confident that you have what you need. Pay attention to any opportunities that might lead you to bring about the change you desire.

The reversed Magician card may also show up when you are on your path to realizing your goal but you have lost your way or motivation. You are struggling with the steps you need to take, and you can no longer see the end result. Perhaps it is time to take a step back, look at what you really need to do, and if it truly is something you want to bring to fruition.

The card can also represent your emotional state. You might feel too confident and take risks without thinking of their consequences. Be aware of the decisions that you make and the actions that you take—they may bring about your downfall.

The reversed Magician may also show up in your reading to warn you of deception, manipulation, and greed. You may have been lured in by the willpower and strength of the Magician and may have begun to manipulate for selfish gain. Or you may be subject to deception. Find out if there is a Magician in your circle—there might be somebody who is deluding you and taking advantage of you.

2 - The High Priestess

The High Priestess is usually standing between two pillars representing the duality of nature—good and evil, masculine and feminine, darkness and light. She believes in the two pillars' equality and serves as a mediator between them. She is at the threshold of two realms, the conscious and the subconscious—the one she protects and guards—and she believes in the importance of finding and recognizing the knowledge in them both.

The High Priestess card focuses on inner knowledge—it is time to put aside your conscious mind and listen to your intuition. She invites you into the realm that she protects—the subconscious—and encourages you to trust your intuition.

The card shows up when the veil between your conscious and your subconscious is at its thinnest. Let the High Priestess guide you into accessing your inner wisdom and intuition; the answers that you seek are in your subconscious. It is the right time to trust your intuition and let yourself be guided by your inner voice. When you need to make a decision, listen to your feelings—they will tell you what is right.

Reversed

The reversed High Priestess card refers to confusion and a struggle to find your inner voice. Rationality is not possible at the moment. You must find a way to follow your intuition. What is it that is blocking it?

Don't be afraid to trust your instinct, especially when you need to make a decision. Difficulties may arise if you ignore them and listen only to your conscious mind. You may feel that something isn't right, and you may feel indecisive about going forward with something. That is your instinct. If you look deep within yourself, you'll find your inner voice waiting for you to listen to it.

The High Priestess card deals not only with wisdom and intuition but also mystery and the unknown. The High Priestess could show up reversed in a reading as a warning that something might be concealed from you that is, or will be, important to you.

3 - The Empress

The Empress card calls you to connect with yourself and discover the beauty and harmony of your life. She encourages you to take care of yourself and listen to what you need in order to find happiness and peace.

The Empress is associated with harmony, bursts of creativity, abundance, and blessings. It guarantees good fortune, and it encourages you to bring your ideas and projects to life; by devoting yourself to them, you will ensure their success. Trust the Empress, and your endeavors will be successful. You might also find yourself in a period of growth. Take a moment to notice the abundance surrounding you, offer gratitude, and look for the opportunities the Empress ensures to create even more abundance.

The Empress could also signal a pregnancy and motherhood —look for other cards that might show this—or a nurturing, compassionate, and caring attitude.

Due to the Empress' connection with nature, she also encourages you to connect with nature. Take a break from your daily life and venture out into the beauty of nature, be it a forest, a lake, or a beach, and breathe in the energy that surrounds you.

Reversed

The Empress reversal shows up when you neglect yourself by focusing too much on what others need. It is time to take care of yourself, too—you have been overlooking your own needs for too long.

You might have also become overprotective and controlling in your relationships because of your nurturing and caring attitude. Your actions may be well-intended, but they may be too much for the people around you.

The Empress reversed may also indicate a creative block with your projects and ideas. You may have worried too much about the quality of your work and perhaps about what others might think of it, too. Creative blocks come and go, they don't last forever, and you'll soon be able to get back to your work. Let your creativity flow and set aside your worries and fears.

When the Empress shows up reversed, it might also mean that you rely too much on others to help you and let them make decisions for you. The card encourages you to trust yourself more and to take matters into your own hands.

4 - The Emperor

The Emperor card symbolizes control, organization, responsibility, discipline, and authority. He values critical and strategic thinking when he plans something. He makes sure he accomplishes all of his goals. When he shows up in a reading, he encourages you to pursue your goals strategically, and you will ensure your success. Organize yourself, plan your steps, and take well-thought-out actions to reach your goals or solve your problems.

You may also find yourself in the Emperor's role—a role of offering security and stability to the people around you, disclosing knowledge, giving structure, and creating rules. The card may also signify the experience and knowledge you have gained and can now pass on to others. You can guide and advise the people surrounding you.

When the Emperor card shows up, it could also mean that you will find yourself in a position of leadership or authority. Use your wisdom to bring clarity and order to the situation that you find yourself in and to make the right decisions.

Reversed

The Emperor reversed shows the need to evaluate your relationship with power, authority, and control and how it currently affects your life. Are you using too much or too little of your power and control? Are you disciplined and responsible?

If you feel you have lost your way when reaching your goals, the card encourages you to take a step back and analyze your situation. Are you committed enough? Have you made a well-thought-out plan, and have you created a routine? Are you disciplined and responsible with your work? Harness the strong and strategic energy from the Emperor, and your endeavors will be successful.

When the Emperor card shows up reversed in a reading, it is also a sign of abused or overused authoritative power that can either originate from you or another person. Find a way to balance the power that you and the others hold. Don't fear the loss of control—too much of it leads only to difficulties.

The Emperor reversed may also show up in a reading to encourage you to stand up to authority. You may have become fed up with the same structure and rules and feel the need to break free from them.

The Emperor reversed signifies a lack of self-control and losing the power he once had when he applied his principles of order, discipline, and responsibility. He now cannot handle the situations he finds himself in; therefore, it is time to rebalance control and power and regain the organization and discipline from before.

5 - The Hierophant

The Hierophant is also known as the High Priest or the Pope in certain decks. He is considered the masculine counterpart to the High Priestess. He is depicted as a religious figure, sitting on a throne between two pillars. Two followers kneel before him, to whom he passes down his wisdom and knowledge—symbolizing a rite of passage.

The Hierophant card encourages you to adhere to an existing system, rules, and certain traditions to ensure a successful result. You are not yet ready to risk establishing a new system and bringing your innovative ideas to life.

The Hierophant signifies a learning period—you might be aided by a mentor, teacher, or guide. He will help you gain knowledge and wisdom and teach you about the system and its principles and traditions. You might also take the role of the Hierophant and pass down your knowledge to others.

When it comes to family and relationships, the Hierophant advises you to take a conventional approach and reminds you of moral values. Sometimes, he may also hint at marriage.

Reversed

When the Hierophant shows up reversed in your reading, you feel constrained by the system you find yourself in and the rules you follow. You are unhappy with the lack of control, flexibility, and freedom that comes with it, and you feel the need to take an unconventional approach. You question the rules and traditions you follow and are confused about whether following them is right for you.

The Hierophant reversed encourages you to make a change and ask yourself if the system you follow is the right one for you. Your life may lack the freedom, flexibility, and control you desire, your relationship may feel stale, and your work may become too restrictive. Others may question your choice to make changes, and you may conflict with them.

The card could also show the need to listen to yourself and not follow advice, which may be unhelpful to you at this time. Let yourself be guided by your inner voice, make your own choices, and create your own path—but be responsible for the risks you take.

6 - The Lovers

The Lovers card mainly refers to a relationship's harmony, trust, unity, and attractiveness. Each of you has built more trust and confidence in your relationship, and you communicate more openly and honestly. You're willing to embrace your vulnerabilities and share them with each other. The bond between you and your partner is strong and unified by your trust, compassion, devotion, and passion. The card may also refer to another kind of relationship with family or friends, where the connection is strengthened by mutual compassion and respect.

The duality of nature is also represented in the Lovers card—masculine and feminine. When the card shows up in your reading, it can mean that you have found yourself in a situation that requires you to choose between two irreconcilable opposing elements.

You may have a moral dilemma about yourself, your life, and your relationships. Consider the consequences that may arise depending on your choice and make the best decision for your situation. Think about what is best for you—choose to love yourself and set aside your worries and fears.

Remember that you can always bring together some things that may seem irreconcilable. Every choice comes with opportunities, challenges, advantages, and disadvantages. The Lovers card encourages you to accept dualities and unify them.

Another meaning of the Lovers card is embracing a new belief system and values. As opposed to the rigidity of an already established system that the Hierophant card encouraged you to respect and follow. You are now ready to develop your own system and rules.

Reversed

The Lovers card reversed shows up in a reading when you are dealing with inner and outer conflicts, disharmony, and a lack of communication and responsibility.

In some cases, when it comes to a relationship, you must re-establish the connection you once had with your partner through communication, honesty, love, and compassion. It has lost its balance, and some issues need to be resolved to strengthen your bond again. In other cases, when communication is no longer possible because of continuous conflicts and a lack of mutual respect, it might mean that you have grown apart. It is time to move on. Sometimes, the Lovers card reversed might also refer to a relationship in which feelings are not mutual.

The Lovers card reversed may show up when you have lost your love and respect for yourself or when you're dealing with inner conflicts. You have lost your balance, and you must regain it. Think about how you can move forward and try to love yourself more.

The card may also refer to a choice you are facing now, which might have substantial consequences if you decide to go forward. The Lovers reversed card urges you to take responsibility for your choices.

7 - The Chariot

The Chariot card represents determination, willpower, confidence, control, and strength. When this card appears in your reading, it encourages you to commit to your plans and goals. Maintain your confidence and determination; be disciplined, and you will eventually succeed.

The card warns you of the challenges you will have to overcome in your endeavors. It shows you the importance of maintaining focus, motivation, and determination to succeed. Be dedicated to your plans and push past any obstacles you may encounter. The Chariot encourages you to take control of your life and each step required towards the desired destination. Trust yourself and know your values.

Reversed

The Chariot reversed shows up in your reading when you lost your motivation and willpower. Either you may be trying to push forward despite losing your direction, or you may completely lose your motivation and commitment. You may be allowing the obstacles that come your way to stop you from achieving what you want—or find the challenges that arise too hard for you to continue. You cannot see the outcome that you want anymore. Take a step back and reassess your situation. Contemplate why you wanted to achieve your goal and find a solution that will help your situation.

It may also mean that you have become obsessed with having control over everything, but there are some aspects in life that we hold no power over. Don't worry about what isn't in your control—focus only on the things that you do have control over.

8 - Strength

The Strength card refers to strength—but not one of a physical nature. Like the Chariot, the Strength card represents strength, will, and power—but compared to the Chariot, these are all of an inner nature.

The Strength card shows up in your reading to remind you that you have enough inner strength, determination, and fortitude to handle what you're struggling with at the moment. You're patient, calm, and confident, your commitment and inner strength are strong, and you will be able to endure any obstacle that comes your way. Be courageous—you have what it takes to persevere—and reach the outcome you want.

The Strength card warns you to rein in your animal instincts, such as strong raw emotions and reactions. You may find yourself feeling angry and jealous and acting instinctively. Balance these powerful feelings and channel them into productive use. In some cases—such as a relationship—you will have to control your rage and be patient, gentle, and compassionate.

Reversed

When the Strength card appears reversed in your reading, you lack inner strength, determination, and confidence in yourself and your abilities. It may also show that you are prone to intense feelings of anger, fear, and insecurity. The Strength reversed urges you to be kind to yourself and find your inner strength.

The card may also signal feelings of unhappiness, negativity, or even depression. It encourages you to take care of yourself and love yourself again so that you can restore the grit that you once had. It may also show jealousy for the people who seem happier than you or have surpassed you. The card urges you to reconnect with yourself and find your inner strength and confidence again.

9 - The Hermit

The Hermit card shows up in your reading to urge you to take a step back and examine your situation. You may need to take some time away from everything—the card encourages you to use it to contemplate your next steps. It advises inner reflection and disconnection from all that you are going through. Deep introspection will help guide you through your situation if you need answers.

The Hermit may also appear when you're considering a new direction in your life. Don't rush your decisions. Reflect and meditate on what the best course is. Search within yourself for the guidance you need, and let yourself be steered by your inner voice.

The card may also appear in a reading when someone will appear in your life and take on the mentor role. He will help you seek the answers within you.

Reversed

The Hermit reversed might mean that you are taking no time to self-reflect or taking too much. Neither of them is helping you.

You may have felt the need to be alone and have secluded yourself so much that you've found yourself lost in your unconscious. You have become so isolated that you have begun to neglect your relationships. Find your way back and balance your inner reflections with your life outside your mind.

If you take no time for self-reflection, the Hermit reversed urges you to find the time to go deep within yourself. You are letting your issues take so much of your time that you can no longer connect with your inner voice. Take some time to listen to it. It will offer you the guidance that you need.

10 - Wheel of Fortune

The Wheel of Fortune card shows up in a reading to remind you that life is constantly changing. You may be going through a difficult time—rest assured, things will soon change. Life is fluid—it is made up of good and bad things, and the constant cycle to which it is subjected is something you cannot control. This cycle of life is governed by the same forces that govern nature. They control the changing of the seasons and the changes in weather, the phases of the Moon, the Sun rising and setting, and the Earth's revolution around the Sun.

The Wheel of Fortune card may also indicate that you are currently experiencing beautiful moments. It reminds you that being grateful is important. Things could change at any given moment. What comes up in your path is always followed by something else.

The Wheel of Fortune could also suggest that a significant change will come into your life. Opportunities may arise that you did not expect—embrace them and welcome the new direction your life will take. Good things await you.

Reversed

When the Wheel of Fortune appears reversed, the card encourages you to wait for the wheel to turn. You may find yourself at the bottom, going through difficult times and seeing no way out of your situation. Remember that it is not in your control—external influences are at play. It is a difficult period over which you have no control and must go through to resurface. Think about how you got where you are now and what lessons you can learn from your situation. The wheel will soon turn, and you will be away from what was once troubling you.

The Wheel of Fortune reversed may signal a change you find hard to accept. Sometimes change is inevitable, and we must accept it to move on. Let the change take effect, and you may find yourself at peace again.

11 - Justice

The Justice card refers to the law of cause and effect. What you will receive will reflect what you have done.

Decisions that may have been made will be judged according to their consequences. You will account for your actions and will be judged fairly. You may have done something you regret, or you may not have acted for the greater good. The Justice card urges you to take responsibility for your actions and to stand accountable when you are faced with their consequences.

The card could also indicate the need to make an important decision soon. Justice advises you to think of the long-term repercussions of what you will choose. Make your choice by listening to your intuition—what is right and wrong—and find a way to stand by your decision.

The Justice card may also refer to a justice that you seek. Justice will be served when the card appears in your reading, and you have been wronged.

Aside from justice and fairness, the Justice card also represents truth and honesty. Before judging, seek the truth, which cannot come from others but only from facts.

Reversed

When Justice appears reversed in your reading, it may indicate that you know you've done something that isn't morally right. You are not willing to accept the consequences. You can hide it, blame it on others, or take responsibility for what you have done and find a solution to correct it. Justice advises you to analyze your situation and acknowledge what you have done.

Correct your mistakes and make better decisions—what you've done is in the past, but it affects both your present and your future. You have a chance to correct what you've done— what you choose now will change both your present and your future.

Justice reversed may also refer to self-criticism. You may judge yourself too much. Learn to forgive yourself and accept that sometimes not everything goes perfectly.

When making a decision regarding others, set aside any prejudice you might have. Make your decision based only on the truth that comes from facts.

12 - The Hanged Man

The position of The Hanged Man signifies the need at this moment to put everything on hold before you take the next step. Either you may need a break, or the Universe urges you to take a break by placing obstacles and difficulties along your way. To progress forward, sometimes we need a pause from everything—this is a time of much-needed reflection that could help change your perspective and notice the surrounding opportunities.

The Hanged Man shows up in your reading to warn you about making rash critical decisions. Postpone what you are indecisive about and the projects whose outcomes you cannot see anymore, and take some time to reflect on the best course of action.

The Hanged Man card represents suspension, patience, and waiting and can signify uncertainty and indecisiveness. He urges you to take a break to reflect on your situation and wait for the opportunity you need. Sometimes it's best to not take hasty and indecisive actions—instead of simply wait. Put everything on hold for a moment and try to see things in a new light.

Reversed

The Hanged Man reversed shows up in your reading when you know you need a pause from everything, but you resist it. Your body and spirit urge you to take a break. Still, you are constantly filling your day with tasks, projects, and activities. Take the advice of the Hanged Man and put everything on hold for a moment. Respect your need for a break and reflect on new perspectives, approaches, or changes.

Another meaning of the reversed Hanged Man refers to your feelings of frustration when you find yourself, your projects, and your life brought to a standstill. You feel you're getting nothing in return from your period of stagnancy. Even though you may feel powerless, understand that this is only a period and that life will move forward.

You may also be stalling for time and not feeling ready to make a decision or a change. The Hanged Man suggests you take the next step—because you may never feel entirely prepared and be pointlessly waiting for a sign that will never come.

13 - Death

The Death card is often misunderstood and feared, but it holds the most positive meaning in the deck. After the pause to reflect, represented in the Hanged Man card, the Death card symbolizes the end of a major phase in your life. It signifies a period of renewal and transformation—a new beginning. Leave the past behind, focus on what awaits you, and embrace this new phase of your life.

Death may also signal a major change that you may fear because of the unknown that comes with it. It may be unexpected, but be ready to welcome it—it is a positive and transformational change that comes with opportunities and advantages.

Death also encourages you to let go of anything that is unhealthy in your life. Be courageous and move forward.

Reversed

The reversed meaning of the Death card also refers to change and resistance. You may find yourself unable to let go of the past and welcome a major change, or you may feel indecisive about the change itself. Your life has stagnated, in need of a change, and you feel as if you are lost in limbo.

Death encourages you to accept change instead of resisting it. Let go of your past and surrender to the new phase of your life that awaits you.

You may also be unable to let go of the unhealthy patterns in your life. Death, once again, urges you to embrace a much-needed change.

14 - Temperance

The Temperance card shows you have the calmness and moderation you need in situations when you are usually anxious and stressed. Even the small things might get to you. It assures you have the balance and patience that are needed in life.

Temperance urges you to consider all perspectives, find a middle path, and avoid extremes. Moderation is vital now, and you have the power to maintain balance and order in life.

The Temperance card also refers to a clear vision of what you want to achieve that you might have at the moment. You are patient and know how to bring your goals to life by taking every step without rushing them and being moderate. Temperance also represents higher learning, meaning that you can adapt to everything that comes your way. Treat it all with calmness and balance, and bring harmony into your work with others.

Reversed

When Temperance is reversed, it indicates a lack of balance in your life that is causing you anxiety and stress. It urges you to make sure that you treat everything with patience and moderation. Think about changes you might need to make to create a better path for yourself and give a purpose to your life.

It may also warn you about a path you might take that will cause you distress. It reminds you that extremes will not help you, and what you need is moderation. Re-examine the priorities that you have in your life and do everything with patience —don't rush your decisions. Sometimes we cannot force things into being, and going to extremes is not an answer either. You only need to be patient, find a balance, and maintain it.

15 - The Devil

The Devil card shows up in your reading to warn you of the negative feelings that have taken hold of you. You feel tempted by the short-term pleasure indulgences offer and don't consider the long-term consequences. The Devil warns you of the cycle of negative thoughts, habits, and behaviors that you are bound in. He advises you to take control by acknowledging their existence and impact on your life. Only you have the power over what you think and do—you can break free from the negative cycle you are currently trapped in.

The Devil may also signal feelings of emptiness and lack of fulfillment that you might be dealing with, aside from feelings of being trapped and powerless. You might let yourself be led by temptation, lust, self-sabotage, and blame others for your mistakes. Regarding relationships, you might have turned your attachment into an unhealthy co-dependency.

Reversed

The Devil reversed shows up in your reading when you can finally free yourself from the negative cycle you have been trapped in. You feel empowered and can now regain control of your life, attachments, and habits. It is time to confront your life's negative feelings and patterns, leave them in the past, and bring about a positive change.

Be prepared to make the needed changes. It's time to permanently end everything that has negatively affected your life—and be ready to take all the steps to self-improvement.

16 - The Tower

The Tower card indicates a major change that will affect you mentally, spiritually, and physically. It doesn't necessarily refer to an unwelcome change in your life but to any kind of fundamental change.

Sometimes the Tower may signal a disastrous change—just like any other change, it is impossible to avoid. We must embrace any change in our way and consider the possibility of it eventually leading us to a better long-term future. Sometimes we must rebuild some things to grow—and the only way we can rebuild is by destroying what was once our foundation.

Major changes that are also unexpected often come with fear and confusion and are hard to adapt to. Still, we must learn to embrace all new changes—the past no longer concerns the present. To move forward, some things must change.

Reversed

The Tower reversed signals the need to make a change. The card's upright meaning refers to external influences that bring about the change. In contrast, the reversed one refers to you acknowledging the need to set aside old beliefs, foundations, values, and opinions and embrace new ones. They no longer represent you; a radical change is needed to grow and accept your new self.

The Tower urges you to embrace the change and warns you about delaying it. If you keep clinging to it, you will end up stuck in the past. To bring about the growth and the transformation that your life needs, you must accept changes—no matter how difficult they may seem.

The Tower warns you about delaying inevitable changes—they will eventually make their way into your life, and their impact will be stronger. Minimize their damage by acknowledging their necessity. The Tower will not let any change go by.

17 - The Star

After the turmoil that the Tower has brought upon you, the Star gives you hope and strength to move forward. This card shows up in your reading after going through a difficult challenge. It reassures you of the power and strength within you and your ability to withstand whatever comes your way and to carry on with your life.

You have gone through difficult times and may have lost hope, but only now can you recognize the true power and resilience within you. You have been able to go through hardships and become stronger and more positive. It is time to heal from your wounds, be optimistic, and move forward. The Star assures you of your inner power and strength and encourages you to grow and aspire to the great things that await you.

Reversed

When the Star shows up reversed in your readings, it means that you have lost your hope and faith and feel that everything is against you. The Star encourages you to set aside your fears and pessimism, your lack of confidence and belief in yourself, and to be more positive and courageous to overcome whatever life brings. Don't give up yet—try to see things in a more positive light, and you'll be able to notice the unexpected opportunities and the wonderful changes that will come your way.

Suppose you feel disconnected from certain aspects of your life and uninspired by your work, projects, and ideas. In that case, the Star encourages you to take some time off and reconnect with your beliefs and values. You may have lost track of what you want in your life and become stuck in a cycle that is now depleting your energy levels. Don't crumble like the Tower in the face of difficulty—trust that you will overcome what you're going through.

18 - The Moon

When the Moon appears in your reading, it means that you're dealing with some old emotions or an experience from your past that you haven't yet confronted. The Moon urges you to deal with the past experiences of your life that might still influence your present and future. Don't let the past project old fears into your present and future.

The Moon can also indicate a lack of clarity that you might have at the moment. You may also feel uncertain—don't make any decisions now. You may not have all the information that you need. Trust your intuition and let it guide you through your uncertainty—not everything is as it seems—and you'll find the clarity you need.

Reversed

The Moon shows up reversed in your reading when it is time to deal with the anxiety and fears that may come from your past. The Moon reversed may also signify confusion and self-deception, urging you to acknowledge and overcome your fears and anxiety to move on. Listen to your intuition, and don't let yourself be guided by things that are not as they seem.

The Moon reversed may also mean that you have started overcoming your past's negative influences. You are ready to free yourself from your fears and anxiety and embrace the positive side of things. You are no longer uncertain and have found the clarity you need.

19 - The Sun

The Sun gives you the strength and vitality you need, abundance, and success in your life. It shows up in your reading to assure you of the happiness that will follow and the fulfillment you desire.

The Sun brings you optimism, confidence, and warm and positive energy to help you reach your goals and dreams. The Sun assures you that things will soon get better if you are going through difficult times.

Reversed

The Sun card shows up reversed in your reading when you struggle to see the positive aspects of your current situation. You may have lost your enthusiasm and confidence. You may question your ability to achieve what you set out to do. However, the Sun assures you that this is only a temporary state—the setbacks you experience are only momentary. You have what you need to bring your goals and dreams to life.

You might have also started to take things for granted. The Sun urges you to find what prevents you from seeing the bright side of things. You may not see it currently, but there are wonderful things to be appreciated in your life.

The Sun reversed may also mean that you are currently over-confident and that your ambitions may have become unrealistic. Think about what you can achieve now and lower your expectations.

20 - Judgment

The Judgment card shows up when you've reached a significant point in your life and when it is time to evaluate yourself and ponder on where you are right now your choices, and your actions. Only through this self-reflection will you understand what the next step is. Some changes and adjustments may be required, small or big, to grow and move forward. Trust your rationality and be prepared to make a choice that will have long-term effects on your future—a life-changing decision may be needed.

The Judgment card encourages you to reflect on your past decisions and actions. Ruminate on your past and use the lessons you have learned to create new and positive changes. You may have already gone through a period of awakening through self-reflection, and now you can see what needs to be changed more clearly.

Reversed

The Judgment card may appear reversed in your reading when you are currently judging yourself too much. You may criticize and doubt yourself excessively. This self-criticism and self-doubt set you back from your plans and make you lose opportunities. Judgment reversed urges you to trust yourself more and move forward more confidently. Set your inner critic aside—it is too harsh with you right now—and try to see your true potential.

Judgment reversal may also mean that it is time for self-reflection. Acknowledge where you are and what lessons you might have to learn to move forward. You have to see your situation as clearly as possible to make changes.

The card also encourages you to forgive yourself for any past mistakes that you might have made and to learn from them. They're only experiences you have gone through, and you must only see them as lessons.

21 - The World

The World symbolizes fulfillment and achievement. You have completed a life-changing accomplishment and proven your resilience in facing challenges. What you once could only envision has come to fruition. The World refers to achieving any major event in your life—a long-term project, graduation, career goal, marriage, and the birth of a child.

The World encourages you to reflect on your journey, celebrate your achievements, and express gratitude for what you have achieved. Take the time to acknowledge your accomplishment before embarking on a new challenge.

If you haven't yet reached this point, the World assures you will soon complete what you set out to achieve. Look back at your progress—you have already accomplished so much. You only need to complete the final step.

Reversed

The World reversed indicates a time when you are nearing the completion of a project or goal, but you have lost your focus and are stuck at a certain point. You can no longer see the steps you need to take to complete your project or goal. Remind yourself of why you undertook that journey and find the last missing step. You will soon complete what you set out to achieve.

The card may also signify a feeling of emptiness and not knowing what you are missing in a specific aspect of your life or a project for which you desire completion. You are close to feeling fulfilled and happy, but something is missing holding you back. You may also need to tie up some loose ends from your past—it is time to let go of it and move on. The World urges you to find what you may be overlooking so that you don't delay a much-needed closure. Make the necessary changes and adjustments and find your way to your desired completion.

THREE

Minor Arcana

WHILE THE MAJOR ARCANA CARDS FOCUS ON THE BIGGER picture of our lives, the Minor Arcana cards deal with the choices and actions that we face daily. They are associated with everyday challenges that might affect us. They guide us through our current situation, offering us insight and aiding us in taking the right steps. These 56 cards portray patterns of thoughts and feelings, experiences, and beliefs.

The Minor Arcana cards consist of four suits—Cups, Wands, Pentacles, and Swords. Each of these suits focuses on various parts of our lives.

The Minor Arcana suits can also tie events to a specific time. Wands represent days or spring, Swords express weeks or autumn, Cups signify months or summer, and Pentacles indicate years or winter.

Cups

The suit of Cups deals with love, feelings, emotions, creativity, and intuition. It often refers to emotional connections and our relationship with ourselves and others.

Ace of Cups

The Ace of Cups urges you to let go of any negative emotions you may have experienced recently and live your life to the fullest. It indicates a new beginning, and, to embrace it, you must let yourself have the chance to start fresh.

This new beginning may refer to new relationships, romantic or of any other kind, which will offer you the emotional fulfillment you need. Suppose you embrace what the Ace of Cups has to provide you with. In that case, you will be given the possibility of growing emotionally, creatively, and spiritually.

Reversed

The Ace of Cups reversed signifies a loss of emotional stability. You have lost the joy that you once had for something meaningful to you. You may feel sad, vulnerable, and frustrated. Find the source of your negative feelings—are they coming from you or another person in your life?

The Ace of Cups reversed may also signify feelings of insecurity. You may be seeking love—but to give and receive love, you must first find a way to love yourself.

The reversed meaning of the Ace of Cups may also refer to a creativity block—you may have lost your motivation and have become frustrated with your progress. The Ace of Cups reversed encourages you to find a way to regain your inspiration.

Two of Cups

The Two of Cups is associated with positive relationships. When it shows up in a reading, it indicates a partnership whose connection is strong, balanced, based on shared values and beliefs, and built on mutual respect and trust.

Regarding romantic relationships, the bond is strengthened by equal compassion, commitment, and love. Communication is more assertive, and you see yourselves as a team supporting each other. The Two of Cups assures you of the deep connection you share with your partner. Sometimes, the card can suggest a proposal, an engagement, or a marriage.

The Two of Cups may signify the beginning of a flourishing romantic relationship or a successful business partnership. The card represents the support, harmony, and trust that will come with your new partnership.

Reversed

The Two of Cups reversed signals a loss of balance and the presence of tension, conflict, and even resentment. The strong connection that was once there to keep you and your partner together is now affected by the imbalance and the lack of communication that worsens the conflicts between you. Be the first to open up, even if it seems complicated for you. Expressing your feelings, discussing them with your partner, and encouraging them to share theirs could eventually help you regain your emotional connection.

The Two of Cups reversed urges you to be cautious when considering a new business partnership. The person you are considering for a partnership may not share your values or goals. You may deal with tension and conflict if you are in a business partnership. Communicate with your partner and try to re-establish the respect and harmony from before. Remind yourselves of the goals and values that you once shared.

Regarding romantic relationships, the Two of Cups reversed could also indicate unhealthy codependency. In a relationship, individuality is essential. Each of you has your own needs and interests, apart from those shared with your partner. They hold great importance for your well-being and your relationship. Find a way to love yourself, too—you deserve just as much love as your partner does.

Three of Cups

The Three of Cups signifies a period of happiness and celebration. It encourages you to take some time off to gather with the people you cherish in your life and to set aside your daily worries. Gathering together, you can give and receive the compassion, love, and support that each of you needs.

The Three of Cups refers to celebrations in all aspects of your life. You may be celebrating a birthday, a wedding, a holiday or a vacation, graduation, a new career, or a job promotion.

The Three of Cups may signal a friendship turning into a romantic relationship or the possibility of finding love in your social life. Social gatherings might bring you and your partner closer if you are in a relationship. They will help remind you why you have chosen each other and help you see how well you fit together.

Reversed

The reversed meaning of the Three of Cups suggests a break from your social life. You must spend some time alone or have lost touch with some of your friends. Appreciate the time you choose to spend with yourself—sometimes you need a break from your daily work and worries and one from your social life. Life may get in the way when it comes to lost friendships. You may be too busy with your work and studies, which may cause neglecting your friendships. At other times, you may grow apart from those who were once your close friends.

The Three of Cups reversed may also signal a period of imbalance and lack of harmony caused by conflicts and gossip. Don't let yourself be engulfed by this negativity—it will go away at some point. Still, if you let yourself be affected by it, its effects will last longer.

Regarding relationships, the Three of Cups reversed may signal the presence of a third party. Someone may be trying to get between you and your partner, or there may be someone else with whom your partner is involved.

Four of Cups

The Four of Cups shows up in your reading when you feel unmotivated, apathetic, and discouraged. You have lost your way forward, and life has become stagnant and monotonous. Certain aspects of your life—such as your relationship or career—may feel dull, or you may be unhappy or indifferent regarding them. The projects that you're involved in are not giving you excitement anymore, and you find it hard to focus on your tasks. The things that happen be they bad or good, don't matter to you anymore.

The Four of Cups urges you to evaluate your situation and to find what makes you feel so unhappy, unmotivated, and apathetic. Try to give meaning to your life, what you have, and what you do—you can find that meaning within you; it had existed once, but you have forgotten it.

You may also turn away new opportunities and projects. They may not align with your plans, or you may be too busy to engage in something new. Don't worry if you're turning away some opportunities—you're not losing them. You're only choosing what you truly need in your life.

Reversed

When the Four of Cups appears reversed, the card refers to your desire for a new beginning. It encourages you to embrace new ideas and projects, new challenges, and new people. The Four of Cups assures you of the opportunities that await you.

You feel inspired and creative and are ready to take on new projects and set new goals.

The Four of Cups reversed may also refer to your appreciation of what you have and the positive way in which you approach all aspects of your life. You are ready for a change or a new beginning, and the Four of Cups signifies your excitement for your future.

Five of Cups

The Five of Cups signifies feelings of disappointment, regret, and unhappiness regarding something that didn't turn out how you hoped it would. Instead of moving on, you dwell in the past and wallow in self-pity and regret. You keep contemplating what went wrong and can't seem to let go of the past. Allow yourself to move on by leaving the past where it belongs —in the past and not in the present, where it will hold you back.

The Five of Cups encourages you to forgive yourself—or someone else if they disappointed you—and accept that you did your best under the circumstances. The only thing that you can do now is to turn your mistakes into lessons and move on.

Reversed

When the Five of Cups shows up reversed in your reading, you have finally let go of your disappointments and regrets and are now ready to move on from your past. You acknowledge and appreciate the lessons you have learned and the strength and resilience you have gained from your experiences. In the larger scheme of things, you may even recognize the value of the hardships that you have gone through.

You may have also suffered a setback in your career or gone through a tense period in your relationship. Do not fall prey to dwelling on old losses and past hurts. It is time to move past these difficult times—you now have what you need to do that.

Six of Cups

The Six of Cups indicates a wish to relive happy memories from your past. You may feel the need to go back to when you were younger. That can happen by returning to a familiar place, such as your hometown or your parents' home, connecting with old friends, or simply reliving those memories in your mind.

When it comes to your career, you may be considering another path or returning to a job from the past. With relationships, a past lover might reappear in your life. If you are already romantically involved and your partner and have gone through a difficult period, looking back at happy memories may bring you the comfort you need. The past can nourish your future, but it's better not to get lost in it for too long—the present and the future await you.

Looking back at memories can not only comfort you, but it can also prevent you from making the same mistakes. Use the past to learn lessons from your experiences, but avoid living in it.

Reversed

The Six of Cups reversed appears in your reading when you are clinging to the past and avoiding the present. You keep going back and thinking about how things used to be, but by doing this, you're missing out on the opportunities that await you in the present.

Remember that you can only change your current situation by living in it and not reliving your happiest memories. It might help to go back to the past and to make sure that you avoid making the same mistakes, but that is all that the past should be—a tool to learn from your experiences. Comfort yourself with your happy memories, but live in the present.

The Six of Cups reversed may also mean you feel disconnected from your inner child or childhood dreams. Think about what you can change instead of just dreaming of what could have been.

Seven of Cups

The Seven of Cups indicates opportunities and choices. You are confronted with many possibilities that seem tempting to you. This card advises you to think carefully about each decision you can make and choose wisely. The Seven of Cups also warns you about illusions and temptations—not all choices are good or realistic. Look deeper into your options and be careful when making a decision.

When it comes to relationships, if you're single, you may be faced with making a decision between different partners. If you're already in a relationship, you may have to decide between love and your career or love and your family. Trust your instincts and choose wisely.

You may be confronted with different options that look appealing to you for your career. Stick to one choice and make sure to commit to it—take all the steps that are needed to make it happen.

Reversed

The reversed meaning of the Seven of Cups focuses on the card's negative characteristics—illusions and temptations. You may be inclined towards making the wrong choice based on your dreams. The Seven of Cups urges you to ground your options in reality and not let yourself be tempted by illusions. Be clear about what you want in your life—choose wisely and realistically.

You may find it hard to make a choice in an aspect of your life because of your lack of clarity. You may lose opportunities and waste time. Think about what you want and make a choice. Sometimes, you might have to act at once to avoid an opportunity.

Eight of Cups

The Eight of Cups deals with change and transition. You may need to walk away from something, such as a disappointing situation, an unfulfilling path, a career, a relationship, or a project that does not bring you happiness. It is time to leave behind what does not make you happy and move on with your life.

The Eight of Cups invites you to rethink your situation. Does it truly make you happy? Does the relationship you're in, or the job you have, bring you the happiness, contentment, and fulfillment you need? Or is it draining you and not giving you the necessary satisfaction? It's hard to walk away from something you have built, but it may be the only choice you have to live a life that aligns with your values and goals.

Reversed

The Eight of Cups reversed appears in a reading when you feel uncertain about which choice you should make. You may wonder if walking away from a disappointing situation is truly the best option for you or if you should give it another chance.

The card urges you to contemplate what would be best for you and to choose wisely. You may fear being alone and decide to stay in a relationship that does not make you happy anymore. You may choose to keep a job that does not bring you the fulfillment you need because of a fear of change. Ask yourself if you genuinely think the situation will improve. Don't choose to stay if you realize it is only draining you and not bringing you the contentment and fulfillment your life needs.

Nine of Cups

The Nine of Cups is associated with happiness, abundance, and fulfillment. The card shows you feel contentment in all aspects of your life, and it may also signify that a wish or a dream of yours is sure to happen. It encourages you to temporarily indulge in life's pleasures and not worry about negative consequences—you have earned it.

Look forward to your future with positivity and gratitude. You have all you need now, and what you desire most will come to fruition.

Reversed

When the Nine of Cups appears reversed in your reading, it means you feel something is missing from your sense of fulfillment. Though everything seems perfect, you're not feeling entirely satisfied with certain aspects of your life. Your life may seem wonderful, but you still feel dissatisfied. Ask yourself what you feel is missing—you may find that it is only a sign of dissatisfaction with yourself.

You may also feel your expectations were not met—something did not turn out how you wished it would. You may need to make some changes and work better towards your goals. Align them with your values, and you will be met with your desired fulfillment.

Ten of Cups

The Ten of Cups means happiness, contentment, and emotional satisfaction in your family and relationships. The card signifies a state of lasting harmony, love, comfort, and compassion. It represents a deep sense of pride and emotional fulfillment.

Regarding your relationship, the Ten of Cups signifies long-term stability, genuine love, and commitment. You and your partner might also feel ready to move forward with your relationship and take the next step.

Regarding your career, even though the Ten of Cups refers mainly to relationships, it indicates a sense of belonging and fulfillment in your current job and a good balance between your life and your career.

Reversed

The Ten of Cups reversed appears in your reading when you seek a stronger connection and harmony in your family and relationships. The card encourages you to rebuild your connection with the people in your life and strengthen the compassion, peace, and love between you.

You struggle to communicate with your partner, and your bond weakens instead of growing stronger. Your expectations for a fulfilling relationship are not being met. You and your partner should both make a change and work better for a loving, harmonious, respectful, and comforting life with each other.

The Ten of Cups may also refer to external influences that affect your relationship, such as relatives that may be meddling in your relationship. Don't let others decide for you what should make you happy—it is only you who knows what and who truly makes you happy.

At work, you may struggle with a temporary atmosphere of tension, a lack of support, frustration, and a temporary loss of your sense of belonging. The Ten of Cups may also signify a lack of balance between your life and your career.

Page of Cups

The Page of Cups shows up in your reading to encourage you to be open to new and unexpected ideas and opportunities that may appear in your life. Trust your intuition, inspiration, and creative self; you will be led to great opportunities.

The Page of Cups advises persistence when you are in a difficult situation. You may have stopped believing in the possibility of achieving your dreams and goals. The only way to face the difficulties is to persist and maintain the belief in your ability to turn them into reality. Sometimes you may also need to change your perspective. Looking at your situation with fresh eyes may reveal what steps you may have missed on your way to achieving your dream.

The Page of Cups may also signify unexpected and happy surprises. Regarding your love life, the card suggests that you may meet someone new if you are single. If you are already in a relationship, you may see it from a new perspective and find appreciation for things you haven't noticed before.

The Page of Cups may also come as a warning with daydreaming. You may set unrealistic and unachievable goals, especially in your career and financial situation.

Reversed

The reversed meaning of the Page of Cups refers to a creativity block. You might lack inspiration, worry about the value of your creativity, and doubt yourself. Rest assured, your ideas are there—this creative block is only temporary—and turning them into reality is worth it.

The reversed Page of Cups may also refer to a person who is emotionally immature, insecure, vulnerable, and perhaps in denial about their reality. This person could be represented by you or a loved one.

Knight of Cups

The Knight of Cups shows up in your reading when your decisions are based on your heart instead of logic. What you feel weighs more than what you think; you are ruled by intuition and emotions.

You are using your intuition not only for your decisions but also for creative projects and goals. You have already dreamed of what you want to achieve and are now taking steps to turn your idea into a reality. Your creativity allows you to see solutions to any issues that may arise.

The appearance of the Knight of Cups in your reading may symbolize romance coming into your life. You feel captivated by the idea of love and are pursuing what you think is genuine love and attraction. The Knight of Cups can signify unrealistic expectations regarding beliefs about true love and how perfect relationships should be.

Reversed

When the Knight of Cups appears reversed in your reading, you're letting yourself be driven too much by emotions. You may be overly emotional and moody. By allowing your emotions completely control your life, you give up on rationality. You may be judging too quickly and jumping to conclusions too fast without first ensuring you have all the facts. You're also avoiding conflict and decisions that must be made, worsening your situation—you should be dealing with your problems. You cannot prevent them infinitely.

The card may also warn you of empty promises and a partner who may seem passive-aggressive. Feelings in your relationship may also suffer some changes—the romance that seemed to be perfect in the beginning was only an illusion, an ideal appearance of what it wasn't.

Queen of Cups

When a Queen of Cups is pulled, she represents a compassionate, caring, nurturing, and sensitive person. She appears in your reading when you are currently embodying her image—you are sympathetic with the people around you. You can support them by showing empathy for their feelings, needs, and problems. You may have become the rock on which others rely when they need someone to confide in and advise them on the best course of action. The card could also point to someone else in your life taking the compassionate and caring role.

The person represented by the Queen of Cups is highly intuitive. She thinks with her heart, not her mind. When a logical approach does not work, follow the Queen of Cups' example—pay attention to what you feel and trust your intuition.

Reversed

The Queen of Cups reversed shows up in your reading when you struggle to sync with your emotions. You may be bottling them up and find it hard to express them. The card may also show that you're currently dealing with emotional instability.

In your romantic relationship, your emotional support has turned into emotional labor. You're giving too much compassion and care, and you receive less than what you offer. You feel emotionally drained—you're putting more effort into your relationship than your partner. This is an unhealthy imbalance that must be corrected.

The card signifies the need to prioritize your needs, too—they are not less important than other people's. The Queen of Cups reversed urges you to take care of your emotional health, too.

King of Cups

The King of Cups signifies a balance between your mind and your heart. You have gained control over your emotions, feelings, and impulses and use your logic and intuition when making decisions. You let neither your feelings nor others' emotions steer you off your path.

With the King of Cups, you can balance and satisfy your emotional and logical needs by using your head and heart when facing different situations. When you're dealing with conflicts and tension, you choose to approach them with calm and logic, and you can restore a sense of peace.

Reversed

When the King of Cups appears reversed, the balance between your mind and your heart is lost. You let yourself be driven by your emotions, and you lose the ability to satisfy your logical and emotional needs.

You may be suffering from a lack of emotional fulfillment. You could be letting your emotional needs take control of your logical ones. You may be selfish and ignorant or let your emotions get the best. The card also signifies that you may feel moody, anxious, or depressed and lack compassion for yourself. It is time to regain your emotional balance. Find a way to control your emotions—seek the cause of the imbalance, understand it, and make a change.

The King of Cups could indicate that someone in your life may be manipulating you emotionally. This manipulation is the reason for your emotional instability. You're dealing with someone else's selfishness and lack of empathy and morals. Find the source of this emotional abuse and rid yourself of its influence.

Wands

The suit of Wands focuses on passion, energy, creativity, and motivation. It often refers to new ideas, spirituality, and our purpose in life.

Ace of Wands

The Ace of Wands represents creativity, potential, and willpower. It shows up in your reading when you feel drawn toward a new idea or project. About which you feel unsure. To tell you to set aside your uncertainty and pursue your passion.

You may have been waiting for a sign to start your project—the Ace of Wands gives you the nudge you need. Even so, it does not guarantee any results. It is only there to help you get started. It is up to you to continue to grow your ideas.

Regarding relationships, the Ace of Wands represents a revival of passion or stronger sensuality. Regarding your career, the card signifies a period of growth and inspiration.

Reversed

The Ace of Wands reversed represents a reluctance to start a new idea or project. You may lack the inspiration, motivation, and passion you need to take your first step and a direction—you find it hard to express these new ideas. The Ace of Wands reversed may also signify a delay in your projects.

Regarding relationships, the Ace of Wands suggests a decrease in passion. To regain the old passion, effort from you and your partner is necessary. The card may also indicate a short-term relationship.

In your career, you feel uninspired and find it hard to finish your tasks or engage in new projects. The Ace of Wands advises you to be patient—these periods when you lack creativity are only temporary.

Two of Wands

The Two of Wands represents the next step that you take after the Ace of Wands. You have already set out to achieve a goal. Now is the time to plan and move forward with it. You are growing the idea for which the Ace of Wands gave you the motivation that you needed.

The Two of Wands also indicates decisions that you may have to make. You may decide to explore new experiences by leaving your comfort zone, which takes courage, but the Two of Wands gives you the confidence that you need to move on. The card's meaning is also about discovery and the need to establish a thorough plan before moving forward with an idea. The card may also refer to long-term goals that you intend to achieve.

In your relationship, you may be considering some changes. Perhaps taking the next step. The Two of Wands stresses the importance of planning to create a new path that will bring you and your partner closer together. You're also planning long-term goals to achieve your dreams in your career.

Reversed

The reversed Two of Wands stresses the importance of setting goals and planning how to achieve them. Think about what you genuinely want and develop a clear path to follow that will help you achieve it.

When reversed, the Two of Wands may also signify a failed plan. You may have forgotten some essential aspects to attain what you set out to do. Patience and a logical strategy are important to achieve your goals.

Another meaning of the Two of Wands reversed may also indicate a fear of putting your plan into motion. You may doubt its success and over-analyze it so much that you're hesitant to start. The card explains that you cannot plan every detail and should be more confident. Be courageous enough to explore the new experiences that await you and to leave your comfort zone behind.

Three of Wands

The Three of Wands shows up in your reading when you are following through with your plans but are considering new opportunities to widen your horizon. This card also refers to creating a lasting foundation for yourself—you have taken the time to thoroughly plan your future. You are now taking each step to ensure you achieve your goals. The Three of Wands may also indicate travel, new adventures, and new experiences.

As you move toward the next stage, you create a solid foundation in your relationship. Regarding your career, you've found new opportunities and the possibility of expanding your options. You may consider working abroad.

Reversed

When the Three of Wands appears reversed in your reading, it shows you are tempted to stay in your comfort zone even though new opportunities and growth possibilities await you. The card encourages you to consider any new options appearing in your path.

The Three of Wands may also signify delays or obstacles on your journey to achieve your goals. You may feel disappointed and frustrated, and you might think that you have wasted your time. The card reminds you that even though you haven't met your expectations, you haven't wasted your time. Your experiences have given you fortitude and have contributed to your personal growth.

You may be faced with frustrations or obstacles in your love life. Remember to be patient—love takes time to grow—and try to understand the need to make compromises from time to time.

Four of Wands

The meaning of the Four Wands refers to stability, harmony, and happiness, especially regarding your home environment. It also suggests celebration, appreciation for everything you have and achieved in your life, and a perfect time to get together with the people you cherish.

The Four of Wands is a card of celebration. It may indicate engagements, marriages, and gatherings; it signifies supportive relationships and strong bonds. The card suggests that a solid foundation exists in your relationship and that the bond between you and your loved one will be strengthened.

When you have worked hard toward achieving a goal, the Four of Wands encourages you to take a break and celebrate all you have accomplished. It is time to acknowledge your progress and hard work before going forward.

Reversed

The reversed meaning of the Four of Wands suggests the opposite of the upright one. You're dealing with a lack of harmony and support in your home environment, and conflicts and tension may arise in your relationships. You have started to feel uncertain about who you really can depend on.

The Four of Wands may also indicate that you may be dealing with hesitation and fear when faced with the next level of your relationship and public commitments of your love. The card urges you to find your fear's source or cause.

The Four of Wands reversed may also mean that you prefer to celebrate your minor achievements by yourself. You're waiting for that last step to be accomplished to feel that it is worth sharing with your family and friends.

Five of Wands

The Five of Wands suggests the presence of a conflict in your life. It signifies tension and even competition in your relationships with others. The card indicates a problem in communication as well—everyone wants to be heard. Still, no one wants to listen to the other. This leads to arguing and a lack of understanding or agreement.

Be the first to listen to others, even if you disagree with what they say. The Five of Wands encourages differences of opinion. What each person says may be helpful when dealing with a particular issue.

You may deal with some small arguments in your relationship, but they are likely not very serious. When it comes to your career, you may face conflicts and find yourself competing with your colleagues.

Reversed

When the Five of Wands shows up reversed in your reading, it suggests that you are currently ignoring situations or problems that would otherwise create tension and conflicts. Sometimes it may help to avoid conflict, but at other times it may make even more issues and steer you away from a solution. Think of conflict as a helpful way to discover the underlying issues of a problem and solve them.

The Five of Wands reversed may also suggest that the conflict or competition in your life has been resolved. There are no more issues for you to worry about. Embrace the sense of relief that has come into your life.

Six of Wands

The meaning of the Six of Wands refers to success and public acknowledgment of your achievements. You have successfully achieved all your goals, and your efforts are acknowledged. You may have received acclaim, an award, or recognition for your work. Be proud of yourself and your hard work—you deserve the fruits of your labor and the recognition that you receive—but try not to turn your pride into arrogance.

When it comes to your love life, the card signals a big chance that you will meet someone. If you are in a relationship, the goals you and your partner have set for your relationship are now coming to fruition.

Reversed

When the Six of Wands appears reversed in your reading, you doubt your abilities and potential to attain your goals. You may also feel neglected, in need of some emotional support from the people around you, and have an overall negative view of yourself. The Six of Wands reversed stresses the importance of regaining your confidence to pursue and meet your goals.

You or your partner may feel overlooked or unappreciated in your love life. If you're single, you may feel you don't receive the attention you deserve compared to others. In your career, the Six of Wands suggests a lack of support or recognition for your work, underachievement because of a lack of interest or ambition, or a failure to succeed.

Seven of Wands

The Seven of Wands deals with the competitive environment that follows your success. You have put in hard work and effort to reach the position you're in now, but others are now challenging it and striving to get where you are. You will have to maintain your position and prove yourself. The Seven of Wands encourages you to hold your ground. You deserve the position you have reached because of your hard work—be ready to stand up for yourself and your beliefs and voice your opinion.

In your love life, you may need to set boundaries or fight for your relationship. External influences, such as family, friends, or other suitors, may challenge and oppose it. You must find the confidence you need to fight for your and your partner's life together.

Reversed

When the Seven of Wands shows up reversed in a reading, you may feel overwhelmed by all the external pressure you face. The challenges that you are dealing with are weighing you down. You may be avoiding conflict or challenges, and, as a result, you are slowly losing your ground.

The Seven of Wands reversed urges you to not let yourself be affected by external influences and to keep fighting for your position and beliefs. Ask yourself if it is worth giving up after all your hard work and efforts.

In your love life, the external forces keep working against the two of you being together, and maintaining your relationship has become more challenging. Alternatively, you may also find yourself in a state of denial and keep fighting for your relationship even though it is not working for you anymore.

Eight of Wands

The Eight of Wands signifies the end of the struggles brought on by the Seven of Wands. This card suggests a high energy level that will shorten your way to achieving your goals. It represents motivation, sudden and positive growth, quick progress, significant results, and positive changes.

In terms of work, apart from rapid growth in your career, quick progress in your projects, or the energy and motivation with which you are working, the Eight of Wands may also suggest a business trip.

Regarding your love life, things are finally picking up pace. You may be met with positive surprises. The Eight of Wands also suggests your readiness for commitment and a need for patience—your partner will soon be ready as well.

Reversed

The Eight of Wands reversed suggests that you might be rushing into things without creating a rational plan or taking all the necessary steps. By doing this, you might make mistakes and create obstacles for yourself. The card urges you to be patient. Be aware of the possibility of your focus shifting. When you set an idea, don't put it aside for another. By jumping from one idea to another one, you're losing your focus, and you end up achieving nothing.

You may feel frustrated because of some delays. The Eight of Wands reversed advises you to remain patient while dealing with the obstacles that appear on your course to achieving your goals. You may want to progress forward quickly, but the challenges you face demand your patience.

You might be dealing with some misunderstandings in your love life. The Eight of Wands reversed advises you to be careful about what you want to say or do. Be patient—now is not the time to push forward.

When it comes to your career, you may be dealing with a sense of stagnation at work because of opportunities you may have lost by not acting fast enough. Alternatively, you may have rushed to attain a new position, and you're now faced with responsibilities that overwhelm you. The Eight of Wands assures you that you will get used to your new responsibilities with patience and time.

Nine of Wands

The Nine of Wands is a sign of resilience, persistence, and hope. The card encourages you to face the challenges and difficulties in your life with courage and determination, and you will ensure your success. You are getting stronger and more resilient with every challenge that you overcome. When your struggles ease, you will notice the strength that you have shown and the resilience that you have gained.

In your love life, the Nine of Wands encourages you and your partner to work as a team through any problems that might arise—love requires hard work, sacrifice, and commitment. The hard work that you both put into your relationship will allow you to take the following steps in your relationship together.

Reversed

The Nine of Wands reversed refers to your struggle to strive towards your goal. You are facing challenges and setbacks weighing you down, and you feel ready to give up. The card encourages you to persevere—what you are dealing with now is only temporary. Trust that the success you desire is much closer than you think.

Despite your best efforts, your relationship seems to be failing in your love life. It has become draining, and you feel like you're the only one putting in the work. The Nine of Wands stresses the importance of both partners working together towards a common goal.

When it comes to your career, you feel exhausted and overwhelmed by your responsibilities. Make sure you avoid taking on a new project or commitment for the moment—you have enough on your plate. Push through for now, and rest assured that everything will ease soon.

Ten of Wands

When the Ten of Wands appears in your reading, you have taken on extra responsibilities currently weighing you down. The card advises you to prioritize the things most important to you when planning your time and to ensure that you get enough rest and time for relaxation. It also stresses the fact that as we advance in life. We are faced with more and more challenges and responsibilities—we must acknowledge that sometimes not everything can be solved. At times, we should also choose not to carry all our burdens ourselves—we can share a burden with others.

When it comes to your relationship, you may see it as a burden instead of seeing your partner as someone who could help you carry your burdens. At work, you may feel burdened by all your responsibilities—the card encourages you not to hesitate to ask for help from your colleagues.

The Ten of Wands refers mainly to responsibilities and burdens, but it may also indicate the nearing of goal completion. After all of your hard work, you're finally taking the last few steps towards accomplishing your goal.

Reversed

The Ten of Wands shows up reversed in your reading to advise you to stop trying to do everything by yourself and to not be afraid to ask for help or say no to things you know you can't handle. You're currently draining your energy level with everything you have to do—don't forget to take care of yourself, aside from your responsibilities. In your relationship, the Ten of Wands reminds you that burdens are meant to be shared. At work, delegate your obligations and remember that your colleagues are there to support you.

There may also be some things that are burdening you, and that may not be necessary for your life. Give up those things that do not add value to your life—don't let yourself be weighed down by what you don't need.

Page of Wands

The Page of Wands shows up in your reading when you get new ideas and desire new experiences or projects. Still, you let yourself be distracted by every idea that comes to your mind. You feel excited by all the possibilities, but you are yet to create a solid plan to bring your ideas to life. The page shows an eagerness to embrace new challenges and experiences, but you may not be ready yet to deal with them.

If you are single, you may feel excited about meeting new people and experiencing new things—the Page of Wands signals you may meet someone. If you are already romantically involved, you and your partner may be open to sharing new things.

Regarding your career, the Page of Wands indicates you might take on a new role at work or a new project. Even if you want these changes, first make sure you are ready to adapt to the extra responsibilities that will come with them.

Reversed

When the Page of Wands appears reversed in your reading, it suggests that you cannot yet create a plan—or follow it—for the many ideas that come to your mind. Stick to one idea and let it slowly become a reality. Plan how you will bring it to life and be ready to overcome any challenges or obstacles. Create a plan, follow it, deal with any obstacles that might come your way, and you'll see your idea slowly turning into reality.

In your love life, you may lack direction at the moment—you may feel unsure about what you truly want in a partner. You are aimlessly searching for something that you don't know. If you are already romantically involved, you may go through a temporary period of stagnation and boredom. Both you and your partner should find a way to change this situation.

Stagnation and boredom may temporarily occur in your career. You might also lack the motivation to follow through with a project or a change in your career.

Knight of Wands

After the unreadiness represented by the Page of Wands, the Knight of Wands gives you the energy, motivation, and passion to follow through with your ideas. You feel ready to take on new responsibilities or complete the projects and tasks that you have right now. You may also feel the need to impress others.

Be aware of any tendency to rush things because of your increased energy level. You may feel impatient and impulsive; consider whether these ideas you want to turn into reality need to happen right now. If you're going to move forward with any of your thoughts, create a thorough plan and follow it to ensure your success.

In your love life, the Knight of Wands could represent someone passionate but impulsive who may also find it difficult to commit. The card can also mean an exciting and adventurous period if you are in a relationship. Still, this period may be characterized by a proneness to risk-taking, instability, and unpredictability.

Reversed

When the Knight of Wands shows up reversed in your reading, you may face obstacles or experience delays in projects that you are eager to complete. These may leave you feeling impatient and frustrated, and you may act impulsively. Try to refrain from impulsiveness and remind yourself that you cannot control everything.

You may act impulsively when accomplishing what you set out to do, rushing through everything and trying to succeed quickly. The card warns you about this—if you continue like this, you may soon find yourself burnt out or far from actually achieving what you wanted. You may also lack direction—align your ideas with your goals and find ways to pursue your passion.

In your love life, the Knight of Wands reversed suggests you or someone in your life may be avoiding genuine commitment. Your relationship may feel unbalanced and unpredictable at the moment; you and your partner may be going through a period in which you are prone to arguments.

Queen of Wands

The Queen of Wands represents a courageous, passionate, and determined person. You may face challenges, but you ensure you achieve your goals by dealing with all the obstacles in your path. You are optimistic and know how to use your strengths to reach what you set out to do.

Regarding your love life, the Queen of Wands represents an outgoing, independent, confident person who would not change to fit anyone's needs. She encourages you to go out, interact with people, and not worry about their opinion. In your relationship, both you and your partner are more open with each other. In this way, you are deepening your connection.

You are determined and passionate at work, and you may find yourself inspiring or leading others. You are filled with positive energy and passion. You can use this energy to support and lead those around you and give them the determination and confidence they need. Now is a good time to advance in your career.

Reversed

Both the upright and the reversed meanings of the Queen of Wands signify a person driven by passion and determination. You may encounter obstacles to achieving your goals, but you have the courage and determination to face them.

You may not be as outgoing as the upright Queen of Wands suggests—you may feel the need to spend some time alone and focus on your feelings and needs. If you have lacked the confidence represented in the upright version, the Queen of Wands reversed encourages you to regain it. Don't worry about what others think; be courageous enough to stand by your beliefs. At work, if you find yourself lacking the motivation or enthusiasm you once had, remind yourself of what used to motivate you before.

In your love life, reversed Queen of Wands may signal selfishness and dominance. You or your partner may have taken your determination and lack of care for the other's opinion to the extreme. Arguments may also spark quickly now. Be mindful of your partner's needs and listen to what they say.

King of Wands

Unlike the other Wands, the King of Wands does not waste time dreaming about ideas but implements them decisively and ensures the success of his goals. He is a natural-born leader with a clear vision of what he wants and may also turn to the support of others to achieve his goals. The King of Wands may also suggest that you encounter an opportunity and assures you hold the power to commit to it and bring it to fruition.

Regarding your career, the King of Wands represents respect from others and longevity in your success. Regarding your love life, the King of Wands signifies a passionate and strong love between you and your partner. Being single indicates a person entering your life who has a fiery and energetic nature and may take the lead in your love life.

Reversed

The reversed King of Wands is not as calculated as its upright version. He may be reckless and make hasty decisions. He may be arrogant, aggressive, ruthless, and dominating when achieving his goals. If you see yourself in the image of the reversed King of Wands, remind yourself that you may need the support of others too, and don't let yourself be arrogant in front of them. Be careful not to set unrealistic expectations either—if you set unattainable goals, you may have to deal with failure. Concerning your career, you may be lacking direction and confidence. Set goals that align with your passion. You may also need to work on your ability to lead others.

In your love life, the reversed King of Wands might signal an arrogant, dominating, and aggressive person who thinks their way is the best. It may refer to you or someone else. This kind of attitude may be coming from good intentions. Still, when it comes to a romantic relationship, a partner should be able to make their own decisions and resolve their problems in the way they see right. Support them, but don't impose your way on them.

Pentacles

The suit of Pentacles deals with material possessions, goals, work, careers, and finances.

Ace of Pentacles

Like all other Aces, the Ace of Pentacles indicates new beginnings and potential. It also signifies abundance and opportunities that will bring prosperity and rewards when invested with your time and energy. The Ace of Pentacles may refer to options such as a new career. Undertaking a new project or idea and the possibility of turning it into reality, or a sum of money that will come into your hands unexpectedly.

When the Ace of Pentacles appears in your reading, be open to any opportunities that might arise—you now have the chance to turn your ideas into reality. The card assures you of the abundance and prosperity that will come with what you set out to achieve.

The Ace of Pentacles symbolizes abundance and fulfillment in all aspects of your life. It signifies a relationship that offers each partner stability, reliability, abundance, and prosperity. The card suggests you can expect a flourishing relationship if you are single.

Reversed

When the Ace of Pentacles shows up reversed in your reading, it signifies a hesitancy to take advantage of the opportunities showing up in your path. You may miss out on chances that could bring you abundance and prosperity. Even so, you should be careful when considering an opportunity—don't make any hasty decisions before thinking about what it will imply and what potential outcomes it might have. Be cautious about taking financial risks—the Ace of Pentacles reversed advises you against them.

The meaning of Ace of Pentacles reversed regarding a romantic relationship signifies a loss of stability and financial concerns. It may also mean you have missed an opportunity in your love life.

Two of Pentacles

The Two of Pentacles shows up in your reading to remind you of the importance of managing your energy, time, and priorities when dealing with multiple responsibilities. You are currently juggling various projects, and you might also be trying to keep a balance between different aspects of your life. The card stresses the importance of taking time to rest—your energy is too valuable. If wasted, it may affect your results and productivity in the long run. Since you're currently dealing with multiple projects, the Two of Pentacles advises you to ensure that you meet deadlines and respect your responsibilities.

Finances may feel unstable at the moment. The Two of Pentacles advises you to prioritize your bills before anything else.

The Two of Pentacles also encourages you to find a balance between the different aspects of your life. Be careful not to neglect your partner or family when dealing with multiple responsibilities. A perfect balance doesn't exist, but adaptability and flexibility are necessary.

Reversed

The Two of Pentacles reversed may signify a struggle to respect all of your responsibilities or to keep up with your bills and payments. Better time management and budgeting are imperative at the moment, as well as self-care when you feel overwhelmed by your responsibilities. Taking a break is necessary when you feel you can't handle everything anymore. You may be juggling too many things at once, and the card advises you to prioritize what is most important right now.

The Two of Pentacles reversed may also indicate an imbalance between the aspects of your life. It has become difficult to juggle your responsibilities, relationship, and family. They may be feeling neglected and alone and may even become resentful. Try to make room for your partner and family—they represent important aspects of your life.

Three of Pentacles

The Three of Pentacles represents a successful beginning of your projects and ideas, and it signifies the important role each team member has in achieving a common goal. Every insight and idea represents a contribution to the project. The card encourages you to see the value each person can bring to ensure its success. This card signifies that all the requirements you need for a project have been met. The people you will work with have the expertise, skills, and experience required to succeed in your endeavor.

At work, collaboration plays an important role in accomplishing shared goals. When it comes to both your career and your finances, the Three of Pentacles can also indicate a period of learning.

In your relationship, you and your partner see yourselves as a team that can accomplish great things together. Collaborating with your partner on various projects can deepen the connection, love, and trust between you two.

Reversed

When the Three of Pentacles appear reversed in a reading, it may suggest that you are currently struggling to collaborate with others. Your team is missing the harmony and respect it requires. Communication is difficult, and the different ideas and insights each member comes up with are not appreciated by the others. You may be dealing with conflicts and a competitive environment at work.

When it comes to your love life, you and your partner struggle to see yourselves as a team. Neither of you should let the other put in all the work and effort required in a relationship. Both of you should work together and see each other as a teammate.

Four of Pentacles

The Four of Pentacles signifies a stable financial situation and a careful approach to spending money. You have recently accumulated a small fortune and want to save it for the future. You wish to maintain your situation and avoid spending money on trifles. The card advises you to be careful about how you see material possessions—you may place too much value on them and become greedy and possessive.

The Four of Pentacles encourages you to examine how you see money. Are you denying yourself even the most minor indulgences or pleasures, and do you desire only to stash away as much money as possible? Do you still enjoy your life while maintaining this particular amount of wealth? The Four of Pentacles advises you to create a balance between saving and spending money.

Alternatively, the Four of Pentacles may signify that by saving money and being careful about expenses, you are securing a comfortable lifestyle for both the present and the future. You have found a balance between saving and spending money.

In your love life, you may be dealing with jealousy and possessiveness. You or your partner may need to work on some past issues regarding fear or insecurity. If you're single, you may not feel ready to love again before resolving some past issues. When it comes to your career, you may have found the stability you desired, but either you choose your job only for financial gain, or you may still feel insecure and doubt your abilities.

Reversed

When the Four of Pentacles appear reversed in your reading, you may have become greedy and possessive regarding money and material possessions. You are being strict and conservative with spending your money. On the other hand, the meaning of the Four of Pentacles may refer to overspending—the card advises you to be careful with your expenses and to balance spending and saving money. The reversed meaning of the card may also refer to generosity—you may be making donations or sharing what you have with the people closest to you.

Regarding your love life, the Four of Pentacles reversed suggests that past issues of fear or insecurity have been resolved. You are ready to love again; alternatively, your relationship does not suffer from feelings of jealousy or possessiveness anymore. Regarding your career, you may be generous and supportive, but on the other hand, you may be setting unrealistic goals.

Five of Pentacles

The Five of Pentacles shows up in a reading when you're going through a period of difficulties. The card may refer to losing something meaningful, a difficult financial situation, debts, or illness. Since the Five of Pentacles is a Minor Arcana card, the problem you are dealing with is only temporary.

The card also suggests feelings of isolation or loneliness—you may be waiting for someone to help you, but you may not realize that help is there if you ask for it. These feelings are especially prominent in your love life. Being emotionally close to your partner and communicating openly is difficult for both of you. The card may also signal financial hardships in your relationship. What is most important right now is for these experiences that you and your partner are going through to bring you closer instead of letting them distance each other. If you are single, you may have given up searching for love.

Feelings of isolation and lack of support may also occur at your workplace. If things can't seem to change, it may be a sign that you have to think about a new career.

Reversed

When the Five of Pentacles appears reversed in your reading, it holds a positive meaning—you have been through hardships. Still, now your situation is changing for the better. You are slowly regaining strength and stability in all aspects of your life. You may have found a new job that values your abilities. Alternative sources of income or someone who may have helped you get back on track or aided you financially. If you have been suffering from an illness, you could be recovering, or you have found a treatment.

Your love life is improving after having gone through challenging experiences. You are now more open to love. Open communication and being emotionally close to your partner are no longer difficult if you are in a relationship. When it comes to your work, hardships have also ended. If you have experienced financial loss, you are now slowly recovering, being able to pay back your debts, and putting money aside for future emergencies.

Six of Pentacles

The Six of Pentacles refers to charity or generosity. It suggests financial help or emotional support. You have learned from the Five of Pentacles what it means to go through hardships, and now you feel the need to help those in the same situation you once had.

Suppose you don't find yourself in a position to help others. In that case, the card may refer to receiving charity—if someone is offering to help you. If you need support, don't be afraid to accept the charity. You'll be able to recover and eventually repay the kindness that was offered to you. You need to be careful not to become dependent on others' help.

The Six of Pentacles can also indicate a supportive, kind, and generous partner. They may offer you financial and emotional support and are ready to help you achieve your goals. You may find someone through generosity that is received or provided if you're single. Regarding your career, your abilities are valued, and you may receive support in achieving your goals.

Reversed

When the Six of Pentacles appears reversed in your reading, it reminds you of the necessity to take care of yourself. You may have been so caught up in offering generosity and charities to others that you have forgotten about yourself and your needs. The Six of Pentacles reversed also warns you about any selfish reasons you might be generous. You should give away selflessly and not try to prove something.

The card may also refer to not receiving gratitude or appreciation for what you have done for someone else. Someone you have helped or lent money to has not given you anything in return. If you are not financially stable, be careful to whom you are giving money—the card warns you about being taken advantage of.

If you're looking for support, you must be careful about who offers it. You may find yourself in a worse situation. They may ask for something that you cannot give in return.

In your love life, the Six of Pentacles refers to an imbalance—one partner may be giving too much. One of you has become dependent on the other, and the other may feel as if they are being exploited. If you are single, beware of this kind of person.

Seven of Pentacles

The Seven of Pentacles refers to investing time and effort. After the end of the hardships indicated by the Six of Pentacles, you are ready to put in the time, effort, and resources required to achieve a long-term goal. You are now looking at the bigger picture of your life. You may doubt whether it is worth putting a lot of effort and energy into something that will not offer you any long-term rewards.

The card can refer to succumbing to a fear of failure. You may worry about your projects not turning into reality even though you have put a lot of effort and time into them. You may be frustrated regarding delays or the slow progress you have made. The Seven of Pentacles reminds you of the importance of appreciating the progress that you have made until now and assures you that the rewards you seek will soon come.

Regarding your relationship, both the upright and the reversed Seven of Pentacles remind you that love needs work to flourish. You may not see the progress yet, but rest assured that even if it is slow, it is constant and will lead to a fulfilling love. If you're single, a friendship may turn into a romantic relationship.

Reversed

You have invested time and effort into something that hasn't given you the rewards or results you were hoping for. The Seven of Pentacles encourages you to take advantage of this experience and to learn from it. Next time, you will know when something is no longer worth investing your time and effort into.

On the other hand, the card may suggest you doubt whether what you're investing in now is worth all the effort and time. Evaluate your results—are they valuable enough to invest your energy and resources? If what you are trying to achieve has only caused you stress and worries, the card advises you to consider investing in something else.

Eight of Pentacles

The Eight of Pentacles refers to hard work, focusing on tasks, dedication, and effort. You are seeking to master your skill or learn a new one—perhaps you are considering changing your education or pursuing further studies. The card encourages you to be dedicated and have patience, and you will eventually succeed. The Eight of Pentacles may also refer to self-improvement or improving different aspects of your life.

Regarding your career, the Eight of Pentacles suggests hard work and dedication. You are close to reaching your career goals, mastering your skill, or learning something new. The card may also signify a promotion following your hard work and effort. When it comes to finances, you will receive rewards for all your hard work; you may also have the chance to become financially independent.

Regarding your love life, the Eight of Pentacles refers to love as a skill that must be learned—treat it like any other skill. You may find yourself falling in love with every aspect of your partner, and you might have achieved the relationship goal that you desired.

Reversed

When the Eight of Pentacles shows up reversed in your reading, you may need to focus more on your tasks and work harder. They may be more demanding, but to reach the desired outcome, you must focus on them and make sure you don't avoid them.

You may currently lack motivation or enthusiasm in your career. Remind yourself of why you chose this job and consider making some changes if you are still unhappy. You may also need to develop your skills and show your dedication at work to be considered for a promotion.

In your love life, the card signals that you or your partner may not be putting in enough effort. You need to care for each other's needs for your love to flourish.

Nine of Pentacles

The Nine of Pentacles signifies success, abundance, material security, and self-sufficiency. As a reward for all your hard work, the Nine of Pentacles encourages you to relax, appreciate your achievements, and not be afraid to celebrate all that you have accomplished. The card also indicates you may have become financially independent through your hard work, discipline, and efforts. Take care of all you have accumulated and ensure you're comfortable in the future.

In your relationship, you and your partner have found a perfect balance between independence and having a life together. You both acknowledge that each has your own needs, interests, work, and social life. They all need to be respected to have a fulfilling relationship. If you're single, you may currently appreciate and enjoy what you have achieved—you may not be looking for someone right now.

Reversed

The Nine of Pentacles reversed may suggest a desire to hide financial instability or a lack of financial security. You are willing to live a certain standard of living even though you acknowledge the importance of saving money and avoiding carefulness at the moment.

You may depend on material comfort to bring you the happiness you desire. You may work more hours than your mind and body can accept and prioritize your financial situation more than the people closest to you. Try to acknowledge the fact that not only material comfort can bring you happiness and fulfillment but also your loved ones.

You may find it hard to communicate openly with your partner regarding your love life. To have a fulfilling relationship, you must learn how to share your feelings and not be afraid to do it. If you're single, you may feel too scared to give up your independence—remember that a balance between freedom and love can always exist in a healthy relationship.

Ten of Pentacles

The Ten of Pentacles indicates satisfaction that comes from the completion of a long-term goal. You are currently enjoying stability and success in all aspects of your life. The card suggests that you have reached the material comfort you desired—you can now appreciate and enjoy your achievements. It assures you of the lasting foundation you have built —what you have accomplished will reflect in the future.

When it comes to your career, the Ten of Pentacles assures you of the financial stability and security your work will bring you in the long term. The card may also suggest you have created a firm foundation for your business.

The Ten of Pentacles also indicates a successful, financially stable, fulfilling long-term relationship. You and your partner have built a lasting foundation and are considering taking the next step in your relationship. If you're single, you currently seek a long-term relationship and value your family's opinion in choosing a partner. The Ten of Pentacles suggests strong connections with your family.

Reversed

When the Ten of Pentacles reversed shows up in your reading, it may signal challenges or delays in reaching the financial security and stability you desire. Your job may be at risk or unstable in the long-term future. You may experience financial loss or conflicts in your family regarding money. The card urges you to re-evaluate your situation and make some changes or decisions that will allow you to regain stability and security for your short-term future and your long-term one.

Regarding your relationship, the Ten of Pentacles reversed signals hardships or conflicts between your family and your partner. You may find that your relationship lacks the support of your family—they may not consider your partner perfect. Try not to let their opinions influence the course of your relationship—you know if you are happy or not with your partner. If you're single, you may be overthinking about the approval or the opinions of others in choosing a partner.

Page of Pentacles

The meaning of the Page of Pentacles is focused on ambition and making plans for the future. It signals new opportunities that will allow you to achieve the material comfort you desire—they may appear as a new job or a new business.

The Page of Pentacles refers to the initial stages of setting a goal. You currently have the energy and motivation required, and, to ensure your success, you are creating a rational plan to follow. The Page of Pentacles assures you of the determination and focus that you will prove on your way to achieving your goals. Now is the time to build the foundation for your success.

When it comes to love, the Page of Pentacles signals an ambitious, loyal, and dedicated person who may enter your life. If you're in a relationship, the card represents strong loyalty and dedication from you and your partner.

Reversed

The Page of Pentacles reversed signifies a lack of focus or motivation. You are currently considering a new idea, but you may doubt your abilities or whether you have enough resources for it. As a result, you may be procrastinating or putting your idea on hold. The opportunity is there for you, but you may be too distracted to take advantage of it. You might daydream about various ideas and your success without taking action on any of them.

In your career, you may feel unmotivated and avoid working. You want to be successful and daydream about it, but you may not be inclined to put in any work or effort. The same applies if you are currently studying.

When it comes to your finances, the card advises you to avoid overspending and save money. The Page of Pentacles reversed suggests financial insecurity.

Regarding your love life, if you're single, the card suggests a lack of focus and commitment for a long-term relationship. If you're in a relationship, there may be frustration and boredom; you and your partner will have to make efforts to rekindle what was once.

Knight of Pentacles

The Knight of Pentacles refers to a responsible, patient, hardworking, and reliable person. When this card appears in your reading, you are committed and dedicated to your goal, and you seek specific results and work hard to ensure them. You make sure that every step is planned thoroughly; you complete all your tasks and respect every responsibility.

Even if sometimes it seems like a routine and your work may feel repetitive, you are determined to follow through with your plan and achieve your goal. The Knight of Pentacles encourages you to stick to what you do to succeed.

Regarding your love life, the Knight of Pentacles indicates a relationship's stability, commitment, dedication, and reliability. You're carefully managing your situation and slowly but steadily building it with your finances.

Reversed

When the Knight of Pentacles appears reversed in your reading, you may lack the motivation, commitment, and ambition required for the accomplishments you desire. The Knight of Pentacles advises you to create and stick to a routine to increase productivity and efficiency and eventually achieve your goals.

On the other hand, the Knight of Pentacles reversed may suggest that you are feeling bored and stuck in your daily routine. Your repetitive work has become exhausting, and you may lack the creativity you desire.

Regarding your love life, you or your partner may neglect your relationship and instead prioritize your work. If you're single, you may be dealing with a fear of rejection at the moment and choose to be alone. When it comes to your finances, the card signals impulsive purchases that could waste your resources.

Queen of Pentacles

The Queen of Pentacles represents a person who takes care of not only the needs of her home and loved ones but also the financial matters. She can maintain a balance between these two and create a caring and financially secure environment. When this card shows up in your reading, you embody the image of the Queen of Pentacles.

Regarding your career, the card also suggests success in all your endeavors. The Queen of Pentacles could appear as a mentor in your life; she will offer you the advice that you need to complete your projects or accomplish your career goals. She is a successful person, and it is through her expertise and caring nature that she can aid you in your endeavors. If you need a business partner, a person in the image of the Queen of Pentacles may appear in your life.

In terms of love, the card signifies a relationship characterized by stability, abundance, and comfort, as well as a nurturing, generous, committed, and ambitious partner. The card represents success, abundance, and financial security in your financial matters.

Reversed

When the Queen of Pentacles reversed shows up in your reading, it shows you are focused on your needs. Create financial security to ensure your independence and maintain your comfortable lifestyle. The card may signify a tendency toward greediness, selfishness, and perhaps even jealousy regarding others who succeed in their endeavors. The Queen of Pentacles reversed could also suggest a lack of focus because of an imbalance between your home and work life.

Regarding your career, you may be dealing with a lack of confidence in your abilities. The Queen of Pentacles reversed may signify an unreliable or jealous person who could potentially affect your work.

Regarding your love life, the card represents a selfish, jealous, and insecure partner. When it comes to finances, you may find it hard to manage your money and become materialistic.

King of Pentacles

The King of Pentacles represents success, financial stability, security, and material comfort. You have completed all your tasks and attained your goals. You have created abundance and prosperity through your hard work and efforts and can now enjoy the fruits of your labor. In terms of finances, the King of Pentacles indicates that you have reached a financial milestone. You have attained financial stability and security and are willing to share your wealth with others.

Regarding your love life, the King of Pentacles suggests an emotionally and financially secure relationship and a generous and caring partner. In your career, you are driven by ambition; you are successful in your endeavors and have an excellent reputation. The King of Pentacles could represent a mentor with experience who will guide and support you in your career. The card may also signify a successful business.

Reversed

The King of Pentacles reversed urges you to take care of your finances. You may be indulging in too much and losing what you have accumulated. You are making poor financial decisions which could lead to a financial loss or even bankruptcy. On the other hand, you may have become too greedy, and you may be hoarding your money.

When it comes to your career, you are unsuccessful in your work projects and find yourself feeling discouraged, unmotivated, and exhausted. At its worst, the King of Pentacles reversed indicates the loss of a job or a business. The card may also represent a greedy and manipulating person you should avoid.

In terms of love, you may be dealing with a greedy, controlling, and materialistic person. The King of Pentacles reversed may also signal manipulation and a loss of financial and emotional security in your relationship.

Swords

The suit of Swords represents our thoughts, words, and actions. It deals with the ideas we communicate, our decisions, conflict, and power.

Ace of Swords

The Ace of Swords suggests a change in perspective and the ability to see all the opportunities that offer the possibility of new beginnings. You are about to experience a breakthrough that will make you see the world around you more clearly. The Ace of Swords encourages you to embrace new opportunities and beginnings and to move forward with your ideas.

The Ace of Swords focuses on creative and intellectual abilities that can bring your ideas to life. It shows up in your reading to tell you now is the time to use them and take action on your ideas. Expect challenges on the way to achieving your goals—but trust your intellectual skills, mental power, and clear vision to guide you towards success.

Pay attention to the double-edged sword represented on the card. It refers to your ability to both create and destroy. The power that you now hold requires responsibility and a set of principles. For example, in terms of finances, choose rationality over emotions.

Concerning your love life, the Ace of Swords encourages honest communication regarding discussions involving essential issues. In terms of your career, the card indicates new beginnings, such as a new career, an intellectually stimulating work environment, and good communication between you and your colleagues.

Reversed

When the Ace of Swords reversed shows up in your reading, it suggests that you lack the clarity required to make decisions. The card warns you about impulsive actions and stresses the importance of a rational approach. Take some time to plan each step and be clear and specific about what you want to achieve.

When it comes to your career, you may have unrealistic ideas, which may result in failure. You may lack the mental clarity required to achieve your goals. Your work environment might also suffer from miscommunication. On the other hand, the Ace of Swords reversed could signal a period of dullness and a lack of intellectual stimulation at work.

In terms of love, miscommunication could lead to misunderstandings or arguments. The Ace of Swords could also signify different points of view that need to be discussed.

Two of Swords

The meaning of the Two of Swords refers to hard choices. You are dealing with the difficulty of choosing between two things—they may seem equally good or bad. There is a possibility that you might be missing something that could help you make the right decision. You should ponder on the advantages and disadvantages of each choice and try to figure out which outcome is the best for you.

The Two of Swords could also indicate you are trying to avoid resolving an important issue or making a choice. The card encourages you to take action or make a decision. What you are dealing with is unlikely to resolve itself, even if you may hope so.

Reversed

You are dealing with two choices whose outcomes seem equally unappealing. What is most important right now is to avoid delaying your situation even further and deciding—get rid of the burden of choosing. You will find a way to deal with the outcome too.

Even though you may see each of your options as equally bad, the Two of Swords tells you there might be something you are missing. It could give you an insight into what you may be overlooked when making your decision.

With the Two of Swords, you might also find yourself at an impasse with someone or in a situation that requires you to take sides. The issue will not resolve until both parties accept the different points of view and are willing to make a compromise.

Three of Swords

The Three of Swords signals intense feelings of sadness, pain, disappointment, and discouragement. The card suggests conflicts, heartbreak, loss, rejection, breakup, or separation. You feel hurt by others' words and actions.

The Three of Swords encourages you to release emotions by accepting and expressing them. Don't bottle your feelings. If you feel sad, let yourself cry. Accept what has happened, express your feelings, and be strong enough to let go of them and move on. Don't dwell too long on negative emotions—heal your wounds and move forward with your life. See your experiences as a way of learning and growing. They strengthen us and teach us what we must avoid in the future.

Reversed

The Three of Swords reversed is a sign of healing. You may have recently faced hardships, but now you are slowly recovering from your wounds. You are learning to let go of what you have gone through, and the card encourages you to look forward to the great things that await you.

Regarding your love life, you and your partner have resolved your issues. You have forgiven each other and are now looking forward to your future together. On the other hand, the Three of Swords reversed could indicate the opposite—you and your partner may find it hard to forgive each other and to let go of old wounds. If you're single, the Three of Swords reversed suggests that you are now open to a new relationship—old wounds having been healed.

Four of Swords

The Four of Swords shows up in your reading to tell you it is time to take a moment of rest. Your energy levels have decreased and must be recharged to undertake the next challenge. The card also tells you now is not the right time to make important decisions—the Four of Swords urges you to take a moment to ponder on your situation. By stepping away from your current situation, you allow yourself to regain clarity and replenish your mental strength.

In terms of your love life, the Four of Swords advises you to take a moment of rest. You may have been relentlessly searching for your partner, which has exhausted you. If you are in a relationship, you may need to spend time with yourself. The card also suggests a vacation for you and your partner.

At work, things may be frustrating or exhausting at the moment. You may need a break— your body and mind need some rest. You may also worry too much about your finances—the Four of Swords advises you to avoid overthinking.

Reversed

The Four of Swords reversed shows up in your reading as a warning that you are close to exhaustion—you greatly need a break. If you go on like this, you will end up burnt out and unable to respect your responsibilities. The Four of Swords reversed urges you to acknowledge when you have reached exhaustion and to take some time for rest. Self-care is necessary to maintain both your mental and physical health. Alternatively, you have taken time for some much-needed rest and have now regained your energy and strength.

When it comes to your love life, you may have come to a point where you end up being rejected because of your endless chase and pressure. To avoid this, the Four of Swords reversed advises you to take a break, rest, and offer some time and space for the other person. If you are already romantically involved and have taken some time to spend with yourself, you may find that this moment of rest has refreshed your love life.

Five of Swords

The Five of Swords refers to conflicts and disagreements. You may have engaged in a conflict and now find yourself regretting your words. If you have won the argument, you may realize that you have lost just as much as the other person. Is your point of view more important than the relationship you have with someone? Is winning an argument worth hurting or frustrating the other person?

The Five of Swords advises you to ask whether a conflict is worth risking a relationship before escalating it. At times, a peaceful agreement or finding common ground is the best choice. Suppose you have lost an argument for good reasons. In that case, the card encourages you to admit that you were wrong and apologize to the other person.

The Five of Swords may also signal tension and irritability in your relationship. Conflicts may arise out of nowhere, and you and your partner may feel the need to argue until either of you wins. It may also fill your environment with hostility or defensiveness at work, which could cause conflicts.

Reversed

The Five of Swords reversed shows up in your reading when all you want is for a period of conflicts and disagreements to end. You want to forgive and forget and return your relationship back to normal. You have begun to realize that even if you won, you would still lose something. Sometimes, the card may also show an ongoing conflict that you cannot seem to resolve.

The Five of Swords reversed shows that the conflict in your relationship has finally ended, and reconciliation is possible. You and your partner wish to forgive each other, move on from the conflict, and find a compromise. At other times, the card may indicate that arguments cannot end, reconciliation does not seem possible, and the only feasible solution is to walk away.

At work, the hostility and defensiveness are starting to dissipate. You have found a compromise. On the other hand, the card may also imply that the conflicts are only getting worse. The only solution would be to bring this up to your manager so things can be handled professionally.

Six of Swords

The Six of Swords refers to a period of transition. You may be filled with sadness and regret at the prospect of leaving behind what was once meaningful to you, but remember, this change is necessary for both your growth and development as a person. Sometimes we must move on from what no longer serves us.

Concerning your love life, the Six of Swords could suggest either an end to your relationship or reconciliation after a period of pain and fights. If you are single, you have finally found the power within you to leave old wounds behind and to look forward to a new relationship.

You may have finally reached the end of a stressful and exhausting period at work. Alternatively, you may have changed a job role or position into one that better serves yourself and your skills.

Reversed

The Six of Swords reversed signals difficulties when faced with a necessary transition. You may not be able to leave the past behind yet, even if you know it is essential to embrace a much-needed change in your situation.

In other cases, you may feel that the transition you face has been imposed upon you and you are trying to resist it. Consider the benefits of this transition and look forward to the new direction your life has taken.

About your love life, you may find it difficult to let go of a relationship that no longer serves you or of old wounds that should not affect your present and future. To live a fulfilling life, we must have the courage to leave behind what no longer makes us happy.

At work, you may be dealing with the prospect of having to leave a stressful and tiresome work environment. Alternatively, you may have to ponder the reasons for the issues you face—are you self-sabotaging yourself?

Seven of Swords

The Seven of Swords refers to betrayal, deception, and trickery. You—or someone else in your life—are trying to be sneaky and get away with something; you also hope to avoid the consequences you would face if you were discovered.

The card emphasizes the risk of being found out—your actions may not be worth the consequences. You may think you could escape them, but that may not be true. If you are the one who is deceived, beware of anything that seems too good to be true or anything that does not feel right.

In your love life, the Seven of Swords warns you of lies, deception, and, worst case, an affair. You or someone in your life may be trying to deceive you, or they may be unfaithful.

When it comes to work and finances, beware of any shady people or business deals. You may face lies, sabotage, and trickery.

Alternatively, the Seven of Swords advises you to take a strategic approach to your projects. Prioritize only the tasks that will allow you to advance towards your goals.

Reversed

The Seven of Swords reversed suggests the reveal of lies, trickery, and deception and the consequences of these actions. It could indicate you, or someone else has unburdened themselves of the guilt they have been carrying and admit their deception.

In your love life, the card signifies the end and reveal of lies and deception. If you are the one who has deceived, the Seven of Swords reversed advises you to admit what you have done before the other person finds out. The truth will also come out at work and regarding finances and the consequences will have to be faced.

Sometimes the Seven of Swords reversed could also suggest that how you have handled your projects until now is no longer working, and you might want to change your approach.

Eight of Swords

When the Eight of Swords shows up in your reading, you feel trapped and see no way out of your current circumstances. You may feel powerless, but the card assures you can change your situation—you only need to see things from a different perspective.

The Eight of Swords may also refer to a victim mentality and advises you to not let your life be driven by other forces but your own. You have what you need to escape—you are not powerless—and your responsibility is to find a way out.

The meaning of the Eight of Swords applies to any aspect of your life in which you face a situation that needs a change. You hold the power to better your current circumstances.

Don't let yourself be passive in your life—if you want to change things, you will have to do it yourself. You likely have many options. You just need to embrace one. You may not like some of them, but what is most important right now is to acknowledge their existence.

Reversed

The Eight of Swords reversed indicates that you no longer have any self-limiting beliefs and are now ready to create change in yourself and your life. You no longer see yourself as the victim. You acknowledge the fact that you have control over your current circumstances and that you can change them.

You have taken a clear look at your life and now see things from a different perspective. You acknowledge the options ahead of you and are ready to embrace them. By taking your current situation into your own hands and not letting other forces decide your journey, you are choosing your path towards a happy and fulfilling life. New experiences await you.

Nine of Swords

The Nine of Swords represents negative thoughts and emotions. It suggests that things may keep you up at night and cause excessive worries, fear, and anxiety. You may feel overwhelmed by these thoughts, and the Nine of Swords warns you about the possibility of manifesting them into reality. The card also wants you to acknowledge the fact that what you fear is most likely untrue, and by overthinking, you may actually worsen your current situation.

It is time to break this cycle of negative emotions and, instead of seeing what could be, try to see what is going well in your life. Don't let yourself obsess over the worst-case scenarios; don't let paranoia and suspicions take hold of you. The Nine of Swords suggests things are not as bad as you see them.

These fears and worries could also be caused by either trauma or recurring anxiety. You may ask for help if you find it difficult to recover from your trauma or control your anxiety.

Reversed

The meaning of the Nine of Swords reversed is close to the upright one. You may still be dealing with fears and worries that keep you up at night. They may stem from your mindset or unresolved issues from your past. Remember that what you fear is most likely only in your mind, and it only hinders you from moving forward with your life or seeing the good things that surround you.

The Nine of Swords reversed also represents a desire to work through your anxieties and worries and to find a way out of this cycle of negative thoughts and emotions. You may realize that what you fear is far from reality and is all in your mind.

The Nine of Swords reversed advises you to seek help and not carry the weight of your worries alone. Others may help you change your perspective and see your situation differently.

Ten of Swords

The Ten of Swords shows up in your reading to indicate a terrible disaster or an inevitable and abrupt ending that could not have been anticipated. The attitude depicted in the Ten of Swords is pity—pity for oneself. You feel frustrated because you thought you had control of your circumstances. Still, now you find out that you actually have no control. The Ten of Swords encourages you to accept the end and embrace whatever awaits you—you may find what will come is better than what has been.

The Ten of Swords could signal the end of your relationship, a hardship in your career, losing a job, or a financial loss. The card may also suggest betrayal or infidelity. You feel pain not only for having been stabbed in the back but also for the inevitable end of the relationship with the one who has betrayed you. You accept the change, but the situation hurts you deeply. The Ten of Swords encourages you to look forward to the future—what will end now will not affect you anymore as long as you let go and embrace a new beginning.

Reversed

Both the upright and the reversed meanings of the Ten of Swords refer to an inevitable disaster. However, the Ten of Swords reversed suggests that you must initiate the ending. It takes courage to give up on something that was once meaningful to you, but a change is needed—what you have now no longer offers you happiness and fulfillment. When the Ten of Swords reversed appears in your reading, it is time to let go of what no longer serves you and move on.

Alternatively, the Ten of Swords reversed may indicate that wounds slowly heal, and your relationships may have another chance. You have gained resilience and have learned lessons from this experience. When it comes to your career, you may have given up on a job that was causing you stress and frustration, and you may have found another.

Page of Swords

The Page of Swords signifies energy, passion, curiosity, and communication. When this card appears in your reading, you feel enthusiastic about new ideas, future plans, or starting a new project. You have lots of energy, and you want to make use of it. You feel passionate about your ideas and want to share them with others. The Page of Swords encourages you to embrace your ideas and move forward with them.

The card also suggests a relationship based more on intellectual discussions than on emotional intimacy. As a result, emotional needs may not be met. Sometimes, small arguments may spark because of miscommunication. Things should be adequately discussed, and neither of you should let any minor dispute escalate.

Regarding your career, besides energy, passion, and new ideas, the Page of Swords may signal the beginning of your career or studies or a period of training. The card assures you that the energy and ambition that resides within you will help you achieve your goals.

Reversed

When reversed, the Page of Swords may indicate arguments, defensiveness, or a failure to communicate, especially in your love life. These could easily affect the harmony of a relationship and may hurt the other person. Most of the time, conflicts are not needed. The card could also signal a person from your workplace who uses their words as a weapon to hurt or deceit.

The Page of Swords reversed may also refer to empty promises. You or someone else in your life may seem eager to commit to something, but they may not respect their promise.

The card could also mean you are not using excessive energy efficiently. You may be trying to handle too many tasks and projects at the same time. Alternatively, you may not use your energy at all. You may either lack direction or have too many ideas for which you still have taken no action.

Knight of Swords

The Knight of Swords represents an ambitious, action-oriented, and focused person who uses their intellectual energy to ensure success in all of their endeavors. They are highly determined and ready to manifest their idea into reality.

They do not care about any challenges that might appear in their way—all they want is to attain their goals, and they do not care about what they might have to do to accomplish them. This sheer determination and ambition might not let them notice what difficulties lay ahead or the unintended consequences that their actions will bring.

If you find yourself in the image of the Knight of Swords, the card urges you to plan ahead and be prepared for whatever might come your way. Think thoroughly about each of your steps before acting.

When it comes to your love life, the card signifies a person who may find emotional intimacy difficult and need intellectual stimulation. Alternatively, the card may tell you it is time to take action—for example, you may have been thinking about a proposal but haven't dared to do it yet.

Reversed

When reversed, the Knight of Swords represents a person with lots of energy but little direction and prone to impulsive decisions. They are even capable of pulling down other people with them. They are impatient and distracted and may be unprepared for what they want to accomplish. They may choose a ruthless approach—they do not care if they hurt others as long as they reach their goals—and they may appear arrogant in front of others.

Concerning your love life, the Knight of Swords symbolizes an aggressive person and even bullying. They may try to impose their way of doing things upon you. The card suggests strong disagreements and conflicts if you are in a relationship. It advises you to move on if there is no way to reconcile.

Queen of Swords

The Queen of Swords represents the power of intellect and mental clarity. You can make judgments without giving in to emotions and are also open to other people's suggestions or points of view. You want to know all the facts before forming an opinion or deciding, and you always search for the truth.

Regarding your relationships with other people, you choose an intellectual connection over an emotional one. Like the Queen of Swords, you are perceptive. You choose to share your views on a situation honestly, without making it seem better or worse than it actually is—because of this, people often come to you for guidance.

When it comes to your love life, the Queen of Swords values self-reliance and independence—you may need to set some boundaries with your partner. If you're single, the card may signal an intellectual but loving person who is selective with potential partners.

Reversed

The Queen of Swords reversed warns you of relying too much on your emotions when faced with a particular situation. The card urges you to take a rational and objective approach. Your feelings are unreliable; they may cloud your judgment and not allow you to make the best decision. Letting yourself be too emotionally involved could cause you to misinterpret your facts.

Regarding your love life, the Queen of Swords may signal an overly critical, coldhearted, manipulative, and resentful person. It may be a current representation of yourself, your partner, or another person trying to interfere in your relationship. These current characteristics may also stem from a recent breakup.

The Queen of Swords reversed could signal an overly critical, bitter, and harsh person at your workplace. This person could be you or somebody else. It may all stem from poor communication.

King of Swords

The King of Swords signifies mental clarity, objectiveness, and intellectual power effectively used to achieve goals. This card highly recommends rational thinking, impartiality, discipline, and sticking to the facts, as well as considering all outcomes when making a decision. The King of Swords encourages you to detach yourself from your emotions when trying to find the truth.

In your love life, the King of Swords represents an ambitious person with high standards for their partner; they rely on rational thinking and masterfully control their emotions. In your relationship, you and your partner support and encourage each other to be your best selves.

When it comes to your career, the King of Swords may represent a vast knowledge mentor who will offer guidance and support in achieving your goals and will challenge you to do your best. They may seem cold and detached, but their help and knowledge are what you need right now. On the other hand, the card may represent you or your current situation. You challenge yourself to be your best self and use discipline and intellectual power to achieve your goals.

Reversed

The King of Swords reversed indicates a misuse of power. You may have become selfish in your desires and even manipulative and persuasive. You might take advantage of others to achieve your goals. The card could also represent arrogance.

Regarding your career, the King of Swords reversed may represent you or another person. They are arrogant and selfish and may use their power to take advantage of others.

Alternatively, the card may refer to a lack of direction and self-discipline, meaning you may also lack the mental clarity required to make the right decisions.

In your love life, the King of Swords reversed signifies a person who uses their intellect to pursue their selfish interests. They may be abusive and lack control over their emotions. If the card does not represent a person in your life, you may risk losing your partner if you do not change your attitude and behavior. Alternatively, the card may warn you of low standards when choosing a partner.

FOUR

The One and Two Card Spreads

A TAROT SPREAD IS A LAYOUT CONSISTING OF SEVERAL CARDS that you use to arrange in certain positions. The meaning of each card differs according to its position in the spread. Tarot spreads are chosen depending on the question and its complexity. The more cards in your spread, the more information your reading will offer you.

There are various spreads that you can use for your tarot readings. As a beginner, starting with the one card spread and the three cards spread may feel less challenging. Before experimenting with these, feel free to use different spreads in your readings. Let's start with the One Card Spread.

One Card Spread

The one-card spread is the easiest to begin with and the quickest when you don't have time for interpreting complex readings. Use it to ask your cards a simple question related to any aspect of your life or regarding any problem or challenge that you currently face.

Think of your question and begin shuffling your cards for as long as you feel it's needed. You can spread your cards and choose the one you feel drawn to. A second suggestion is to place your deck down and, while still holding it, choose a card from where a gap forms in the pile. Another option is to cut your deck into two piles and choose the first card.

It may sometimes happen that a card jumps out of your deck while shuffling. If you feel drawn to it, the answer to your question lies in its meaning.

Example of questions for one card tarot spreads:

Yes or no:

Will I get this position?

Is this individual I met going to become a serious relationship for me?

Direction:

What's the best approach to take this relationship to the next stage?

What do I need to know now?

Looking for facts:

Encouragement and affirmation of what you previously knew

How does my lover/employer/friend/ feel about me?

What do I need to recognize about a situation?

Two Card Spread

Two cards spreads are excellent for this-or-that situations when confronted with a choice. Based on the card in either position 1 or 2, evaluate how each card makes you feel intuitive.

Example of questions for two card tarot spreads:

Should I move or stay in my existing home?

Should I leave or remain at my present job?

Should I travel to (insert destination) this vacation?

FIVE

Three Card Spread

Although a three-card reading is relatively simple, it provides enough insight into your situation, be it a complex one or not. Using this spread, you shuffle your cards and pull three out of your deck. You lay them out in the order that you picked them. Each card will represent a specific insight into your question. The following are a few classic three-card spreads, but as you become more used to tarot readings, you can create your own three-card spread.

Past-Present-Future Tarot Spread

In this spread, the first card you pull represents past influences—elements from the past that are currently affecting your situation.

The second card may show you the situation you asked about or what present influences exist.

The third card offers insight into the most likely outcome of your current situation if things stay on the path they are on.

This spread helps you understand why you currently find yourself in the situation presented by the second card. The first card gives you an insight into the elements from your past that have affected it. It also helps you make choices and decisions based on what the third card shows you. If the outcome is undesirable, make some changes to your current situation, or be careful with your decisions moving forward.

Career Spread

Use this spread to evaluate your career.

In this spread, the first card represents your present position.

The second card may show you the situation stopping you.

The third card shows you how to move forward.

Mind-Body-Spirit Tarot Spread

This spread is used when you need insight into the balance your life requires now and is helpful for self-discovery. It can help you clarify your emotions and needs and advise you on what changes you might need to make. Each card offers unique insights into your situation, depending on your needs.

The first card, representing your mind, offers you a glimpse into what you might need to do to change your thought patterns and feelings and improve your rationality. You may feel sad, helpless, frustrated, confused, angry, impatient, or lost —the card will tell you what changes you might need to make.

The second card advises you on what you need to do for your body—what your physical health requires at the moment.

The third card refers to spiritual growth, what your soul needs at this moment, and your desires.

Situation-Obstacle-Advice/Outcome Tarot Spread

This spread is most useful when you need insight into a specific situation or when dealing with a conflict that needs to be resolved.

The first card that you pull represents your situation at this moment.

The second card signifies the obstacle or the challenges that you need to overcome. It may show you the cause of the conflict you are currently dealing with.

The third card shows you either a piece of advice or the most probable outcome.

Three Card Love Spread

Three card tarot spreads can be used for love readings. Choose what each of the three cards that you pull represents.

In a traditional three-card love spread, the first card represents you, the second one your partner, and the third one can represent the current state of your relationship, its potential, or its dynamics.

The first card, which represents you, describes your role in your relationship, how you perceive yourself, and how that may affect your relationship.

The second card, representing your partner, follows the same pattern—it describes their role, how you perceive them, and how that may affect your relationship.

The third card can either describe the characteristics of your relationship or show you the current state in which you and your partner find yourselves.

SIX

Five Card Spread

Five-card tarot spreads offer insight into various situations you might be dealing with concerning things such as life, career, love, or family. They can even help you with decision-making. To use this spread, you can either place all the cards in a single row or lay them out in the shape of a cross. Place three cards in a row, one above the second and another below it. Or lay them out as a horseshoe, placing a single card at the top, two below it on opposite sides, and then two more below. Depending on your needs, you can choose what each card represents.

One five-card spread you could use for your reading is similar to the three-card one—concerning the past, present, and future. Place the first three cards you pull in a row to use this spread. They will represent your past and current situation and the most likely outcome if things don't change.

Below the card representing the past, place the fourth card. It will show you what is holding you back from moving forward—there may be some elements from your past that don't allow you to take the next steps. You will have to acknowledge and address them to move forward.

Below the card representing the future, place the fifth card, which will offer you guidance regarding the next steps in your life.

Pentagram Spread

The Pentagram spread consists of a layout of 5 cards laid out in the shape of a 5-point star.

The first card is placed at the top of the pentagram, whose meaning concerns an origin—the cause of the issue asked.

The second card is placed on the lower left, representing a destination—where your path will take you if you make no changes to your current situation.

The third card is placed in the middle, on the right side, and its meaning concerns challenges or obstacles you must confront to accomplish what you want.

The fourth card is in the middle, on the left side, and its role is to clarify your question—what you're aware of and what you need to know about your current situation.

The fifth card is placed on the opposite side of the second one, on the lower right. This card represents your goal—what you want to accomplish—and tells you what changes you need to make to get past your issue.

Five Card Love Spread

The five-card love spread is similar to the three-card one. Still, it offers you more insight into your relationship—as we've said before, the more cards in your reading, the more information they will provide you with.

Like in the three-card love spread, the first card (in the row of three cards) represents your role in the relationship and your perspective. In comparison, the second one (the last one in the row of three cards) represents your partner's role and perspective.

The third card (which is the second one in the row of three cards) refers to the past. The foundations of your relationship, how it started, and what united you and your partner.

The fourth card (placed at the top of your spread) represents the current state of your relationship, its dynamics, and, if it's the case, the issues you and your partner are dealing with.

The fifth card (at the bottom of your spread) offers insight into how your relationship will evolve if nothing changes—the most likely outcome.

Compatibility Tarot Spread

The first card represents your feelings about the relationship

The second card represents your partner's feelings about the relationship

The third card represents the dominant characteristic of the relationship dynamic (place in the center)

The fourth card represents the challenges or conflicts influencing the dominant aspect of the relationship. Place below the third card.

The fifth card represents the potential of the relationship. Place above the third card.

Fork in the Road

An excellent spread to help you evaluate two decisions and their possible outcomes.

The first card represents your decision or journey.

The second card is the first option presented to you.

The third card represents the outcome of option 1.

The fourth card is the second option presented to you.

The fifth card represents the outcome of option 2.

SEVEN

More Spreads

Relationship Tarot Spread

STARTING FROM THE TOP AND READING THE CARDS FROM LEFT to right, the first card shows your relationship in the present time.

The second card represents your feeling toward the relationship and your partner at the present time.

The third card represents your partner's feelings within the relationship. Let this card give you an overall understanding that can be used for the most significant outcome.

The fourth card represents potential obstacles and blocks you may face in your relationship or that no longer serve your relationship. Any emotional crisis, position, or conflict stops you from going forward quickly.

The fifth card represents the best way to proceed forward to unstick those rough blocks or hurdles that may not provide your relationship.

The sixth and final card shows you likely insight into the outcome of the relationship as it is in the present juncture, as cards one through five have indicated.

The Seven Card Horseshoe Spread

Each card in this seven-card spread represents the various aspects of the issue or situation in your question. The cards in this spread are arranged in the shape of a horseshoe, which can be laid out either with the open or the open end.

The first card in the horseshoe spread represents the past elements currently affecting your situation.

The second card describes your current situation—what you're dealing with at the moment.

The third card represents hidden influences—what you may be overlooking or not know about currently influencing your situation. You may not be aware of the difficulties, conflicts, or opportunities that play an important role in your situation.

The fourth card shows you the attitude you have towards your situation. It may be a positive card, suggesting you might feel hopeful or excited, or a negative card, indicating you might feel worried, fearful, or skeptical.

The fifth card represents the influences that come from others. Are the other people in your life supporting you or holding you back from your endeavors? Are you letting yourself be affected by these external influences?

The sixth card offers you guidance for your current situation by showing you the best course of action you should take.

The seventh card shows you the most probable outcome of your situation if things don't change.

Celtic Cross Tarot Spread

Although it is not considered an easy spread for beginners, it is an excellent spread for readings that concern complex questions and general information. The Celtic cross tarot spread consists of 10 cards—the first six of them are laid out in the shape of a cross. The rest of the 4 cards are laid out in a column next to the cross, placed from the bottom to the top, starting with the seventh card.

The first six cards deal with your current situation, issue, cause, and where it will take you. The other four cards help you better understand your situation and the changes you can make.

The first card, in the middle of the cross, represents your current situation.

The second card is placed on top of the first one, crossing it diagonally. It shows you the first challenge or obstacle you will face when addressing the issue you are dealing with.

The third card at the bottom of the cross shows you the foundations of the issue you are asking about that originates from the distant past.

The fourth card, placed on the left side of the cross, represents events from the recent past that are affecting your situation.

Placed at the top of the cross, the fifth card refers to the future you are trying to manifest into reality.

The sixth card, on the right side of the cross, refers to the near future and events related to your issue that will soon come into being.

The following four cards in your spread, laid out in a column starting from the bottom, indicate the following: internal influences (such as the attitude that you have towards your situation and the power that you hold over your issue), external influences (how much the attitudes of the people around you affect your situation), hopes or fears that you might have, and the most likely outcome of your situation.

Birthday Spread

Birthday tarot spreads consist of cards showing you what you would like to know regarding your past year and your next year. You can choose to use either only the Major Arcana (for broader insights) or the Minor Arcana (for more detailed insights).

Here is an example of a birthday tarot spread that consists of 10 cards:

The first card will offer insight into the most important lessons from your past year.

The second card will show you your main aspirations, goals, or wishes for the next year.

The third card will give you insight into what will need to be done to reach your dreams and aspirations or accomplish your goals.

The fourth card will show you what challenges or obstacles you might encounter to achieve your goal or fulfill your wish.

The fifth card will give you insight into your emotional journey in the next year and may refer to relationships and personal achievements.

The sixth card will show you what lies ahead for your health and well-being.

The seventh card will refer to what your career and work will look like in the coming year and your finances.

The eighth card will show your spiritual journey over the next year—your energy and inner fulfillment.

The ninth card will give you insight into what you should focus on the following year.

The tenth card will show you the most important lesson you will learn in the year ahead.

Cross and Triangle Spread

This tarot spread, made up of nine cards, is used for questions regarding the overall direction of your life. Place the following cards in a row: the second card, the first, the fourth, the ninth, and the eighth. On the left side of the first card, place the fifth card, then on its right side, put the third card. On the left side of the eighth card, place the sixth card, and on its right side, place the seventh card.

The first card refers to the force that drives your life.

The second card indicates the influence that affects your thoughts.

The third card shows you the influence over your emotions.

The fourth card indicates what influence exists that affects your spiritual self.

The fifth card specifies the influence over your physical self.

The sixth card shows what internal influences affect your life.

The seventh card offers the external influences standing in your way or holding you back.

The eighth card shows you insight into what changes you need to make.

The ninth card indicates the most likely outcome of your situation if you let things stay the same.

Ten Card Love Spread

This ten-card tarot spread is used for more in-depth love readings. The first five cards are placed in a row. The sixth card is placed above the third one, and the seventh and eighth cards are placed below the row of five in the middle. Then the ninth and the tenth are placed above the sixth one, on opposite sides, like a horseshoe made up of three cards with the open end.

The first card represents the influences from the distant past that might affect your relationship.

The second card refers to recent events that influence your relationship.

The third card refers to the current situation in which you and your partner find yourselves.

The fourth card shows influences that might appear in your future and affect your relationship.

The fifth card represents the influences from other people you and your partner might let affect your relationship. Other external elements, such as finances, might also show up that could influence you and your partner's situation.

The sixth card represents your perspective on your relationship, feelings, and beliefs that you might not know yet.

The seventh card shows you the good energy that drives your partnership.

The eighth card offers insight into what might be troubling your relationship—the elements working against you and your partner.

The ninth card presents hopes and fears you have related to your relationship.

The tenth card shows you the most probable outcome of your relationship if things stay the same.

The Romany Spread

The Romany spread can offer you a lot of information when looking for an overview of your situation or solutions to issues you might be dealing with. This spread consists of 21 cards laid out in three rows. The first row refers to the past, the second one to the present, and the third one to the future.

You can either only read the past, present, and future aspects that the cards in each row show, or you can give meaning to each of the seven columns of the spread for a more detailed reading. For example, the first column comprises the first, the fifth, and the eighth cards.

The first column refers to you and the most important elements in your life at this moment. It may present the situation you've asked about or some elements related to it you haven't thought of yet.

The second column, the second, the ninth, and the sixteenth cards represent your relationships. This includes your partner, family, friends, or co-workers and how they may influence your situation or issue.

The third column—the third, the tenth, and the seventeenth cards—indicates your hopes and dreams and fears and worries.

The fourth column includes the fourth, the eleventh, and the eighteenth cards. This column indicates factors—such as plans, projects, mistakes, and failures—that you're aware of and that influence your situation but perhaps you haven't thought of. These cards offer clarity regarding the elements currently affecting your case.

The fifth column—which consists of the fifth, the twelfth, and the nineteenth cards—indicates unexpected events and developments that might occur.

The sixth column—made up of the sixth, the thirteenth, and the twentieth cards—shows you the forthcoming events in your life over the next few months.

The seventh column—the seventh, the fourteenth, and the twenty-first cards—shows you the most likely long-term outcome in relation to your situation. If it greatly differs from what the cards in the sixth column show, it may imply an unexpected turn of events.

Astrological Spread

This tarot spread uses the 12 astrological houses—considered the 12 aspects of a person's life—and it's suitable for both general and detailed questions. The cards are laid up in the shape of a clock.

The first card in this spread features the first astrological house, associated with the zodiac sign Aries. It represents your identity—it describes how you see yourself, how others see you, your personality, and your attitude regarding your life.

The second card is associated with Taurus and resources. It shows everything that concerns money and possessions. It also shows your self-worth, priorities, and values.

The third card is represented by Gemini and refers to communication and your surroundings. The environment in which you live and the people with whom you have a mild relationship, but not those with whom you are in a very close relationship.

The fourth card is associated with Cancer and refers to family and your home. It deals with the close relationships in your life and your home environment.

The fifth card is represented by Leo, and it concerns your creativity in all aspects of your life. It not only refers to creativity in hobbies or projects but also to everything you create and how you solve your problems. The card also concerns your love life and how you deal with your emotions.

The sixth card is associated with Virgo, work, and your daily routine. It deals with your health, taking care of yourself, habits and daily activities, and responsibilities.

The seventh card is represented by Libra and concerns your relationships. Your romantic partner, business partner, friends, even your enemies), how you interact with others and your attitude towards your partnerships.

The eighth card is associated with Scorpio and deals with the elements in everyone's life that are hard to talk about, such as money, taxes, inheritances, death, sex, and major changes.

The ninth card is represented by Sagittarius and refers to growth—expanding your mind (your perspective), knowledge, and belief systems.

The tenth card is associated with Capricorn and deals with your career, financial status, reputation, and social responsibilities.

The eleventh card is represented by Aquarius, and it concerns your social life—how you interact with the world.

The twelfth card is associated with Pisces and deals with your subconscious mind. It shows your dreams, fears, worries, burdens, and difficulties you might be dealing with, limitations and restrictions you might be imposing on yourself, or how you deal with your potential.

EIGHT

Choosing Your Deck

THERE IS NO RULE ABOUT CHOOSING YOUR DECK. THE RIGHT one for you is the one with which you feel a connection—trust what your intuition tells you.

There are now hundreds of options for tarot decks, which may feel daunting when faced with choosing one. Each deck's illustration style, symbolism, and energy differs and may evoke different feelings through their readings—each has a distinct voice. You may find some online previews of the cards—research them before buying a deck—and if you feel the cards speak to you, you'll know which deck is the right one for you.

Sometimes we may only discover if a deck is right for us when we start using it. Therefore, when choosing a tarot deck, what would be best is to research the imagery of the cards. What is your first reaction to them? Think about what you like about them—the colors, the theme, the illustrations. Do you feel as if the cards speak to you? Are their meanings easily understood by looking at their images? It is in the imagery of the cards that we discover their meaning and through which we can interpret the story they depict.

You should feel your intuition flow when you look at the imagery of the cards. If they have the power to inspire you and give meaning to what you see—they may as well be the cards you need for your readings.

When you look at the imagery of a specific deck, you should be able to tap into your intuition. Our intuition lies in our subconscious, that part of our mind that gathers all the information from our senses and is hidden from our conscious. Our subconscious mind communicates with our conscious mind through intuition. Tarot gives us the possibility of accessing what hides in our subconscious.

Suppose you find it hard to choose your first tarot deck. In that case, you could start with the most popular one, the Rider-Waite deck, whose illustrations are straightforward, relatable, and easy to understand and interpret.

When choosing a tarot deck, you should also consider the size of the cards. You can find large, regular, and small decks. It could be hard to shuffle large-sized cards, but maybe you prefer the illustrations bigger. Traditional decks are suitable for personal readings or when you read for someone else. Small decks are the best when you want to carry them with you or if you'd like to travel with them. Choose the size that best fits your needs.

There is also a common misconception that tarot decks have to be given as a gift and that you cannot buy your own. Don't let that stop you from buying the cards you want—if you feel connected to a specific tarot deck, you can buy it yourself and use it. It doesn't have to be gifted to you. What matters most is not the source of the deck—it could have either been given to you or bought by you—but the connection you have with it.

NINE

Care for Your Cards

TREAT YOUR TAROT DECK LIKE A CLOSE FRIEND. PROTECT IT BY wrapping it into a fabric of your choice. If it came with a box, you could also choose to keep your cards in it. Always keep them in either a cloth or a box, especially if you carry your deck or travel with it. Make sure you take care of your cards and protect them from debris.

Your deck should also only be handled by you. Each of us has a kind of energy, and your tarot cards recognize yours. The deck itself holds an energy that connects with yours. If your cards are touched by somebody else, cleanse your deck of any residual energy left by them. Otherwise, your readings will be affected by it.

When your cards are cleansed, your readings are more accurate and precise. Before doing tarot readings, especially before a first reading, cleanse your cards. When you do more and more readings, your cards will need cleansing again. They accumulate what one may call "debris" from the emotional weight that remains after every reading. Energy and intention from previous readings may also be left in your cards—feelings, such as sadness, may linger. Your new reading should be fresh, free of all the previous energy you put into your cards. Think about cleansing as a way to "reset" your cards.

By cleansing your deck, you ensure the accuracy of your readings. Although there are no rules regarding how often you should cleanse your cards—use your intuition for this—it is recommended that you cleanse your deck every time you do a reading. Cards also need cleansing if someone else uses your deck. Also, do readings for others. If you haven't used your cards in a while, after traveling—your deck may pick up energy from the places you went to—or if the connection between you and your cards feels weaker or you feel it's time to cleanse them.

When you get a new tarot card deck, cleanse it—it is charged with energy from all the people that have handled it before you. There are different ways to cleanse your cards, and you can choose to do it in the way that feels right to you.

Consider cleansing them for a new tarot deck by sorting and shuffling the cards. Doing this can also help you form a connection with your new cards. Begin by laying out your cards, starting with the Major Arcana and then the Minor Arcana. Take your time to analyze their illustrations—what do they want to portray? Is there a story hidden in them? Then mix all of them—don't think about it; mix them randomly and chaotically—and shuffle them.

Another way to cleanse your cards is by visualization. Hold the deck in your hands, close your eyes, and imagine a white light surrounding it, clearing it of all the unwanted energy.

You can cleanse your cards with crystals such as clear quartz. It helps access higher consciousness and amplifies energy. Selenite improves clarity. Amethyst enhances your intuition and wisdom and heightens your awareness. Moonstone helps you access your inner wisdom and strengthen your intuition.

Place the crystal on top of the deck. Depending on the shape of the crystal, place the deck on it, and let it charge the cards.

You can also choose a crystal that corresponds with the reading that you want to do. For example, select rose quartz, lapis lazuli, onyx, or peridot for a relationship reading. For questions regarding obstacles, you need to overcome, use a moonstone, obsidian, fluorite, or quartz. For challenges or difficulties, use malachite, smoky quartz, or onyx.

Another way to cleanse your cards is by smoke. There is a variety of herbs, incense, and wood that can be used. Carefully hold your deck over herbal incense smoke—such as lavender, which aids in clear communication, or sage, which dispels negativity—or a dried wand.

Like crystals, you can also cleanse your tarot cards by leaving them on a windowsill in the moonlight. This is best done when it is a full moon, as the energy from the moon is at its strongest during that phase.

Tarot cards can also be cleansed by leaving them in a bowl of salt—which is a powerful cleanser—for a few hours. Make sure that the bowl is placed in a dry place.

Other simple ways would be to thoroughly shuffle your cards or cleanse your cards by knocking on your deck three times. Think of the knocking as a way to clear the cards of all the energy they have accumulated by knocking them out.

Conclusion

We have learned the basics of tarot reading, the spreads we can use, explained each of the Major Arcana and Minor Arcana cards, and discussed how to choose and care for our deck. It may have all seemed daunting initially, but now you have everything you need to start your tarot reading journey.

We have learned that tarot cards depict everyday human experiences, feelings, and thoughts. We use universal interpretations, personal perceptions, and intuition to interpret their meanings. The cards help us gain insight into our lives, current situations, the world, and the people around us. They give us solutions to problems and advice on overcoming the challenges we might face in the future.

We know tarot cards cannot tell us the exact future, but they offer insight into all potential outcomes. It all comes down to our choices, and the cards help us evaluate our situation and make better decisions to ensure our path is the one we desire.

You know now that you can find the hidden meanings in each tarot card by tapping into your intuition and using it to decipher their illustrations. You can understand the universal

Conclusion

interpretations of the cards and know how to use them alongside your intuition to figure out what they try to tell you regarding your situation.

We have learned about each card's energy and understand the significance of developing a deep connection with your deck. You know how to care for your tarot cards and understand the importance of cleansing your deck, especially one you have just bought.

You have discovered that the Major Arcana cards deal with the bigger picture of our lives and the Minor Arcana cards refer to temporary situations and daily challenges. You have learned that the Fool is the character that undertakes the journey illustrated in the Major Arcana cards and what each of the suits of the Minor Arcana represents.

It is now time to delve into the world of tarot and do your first reading. Remember the most important thing we have discussed—develop a deep connection with your tarot deck and try to use your intuition when reading your cards. Acknowledge the energy each of the cards holds and listen to it. Look at the illustration and seek the meaning hidden in it. You will find that each card will speak to you if you listen to them. Embrace the energy of your deck, and you will gain insight into any aspect of your life.

What is the first question you would like to ask your tarot cards?

If you're looking for more divination tools, take a peek at Divination with Stones: A Beginner's Guide to Lithomancy, book 5 in the Divination Magic for Beginners series.

References

A Brief History of Tarot Cards. (n.d.). Bicycle Playing Cards. https://bicyclecards.com/article/a-brief-history-of-tarot-cards/

Bunning, J. (n.d.). Lesson 1 - Introduction to the Tarot. Learning the Tarot. http://www.learntarot.com/less1.htm

Cross and Triangle Spread. (n.d.). Crystal Clear Reflections. https://crystal-reflections.com/tarot3/spreads/cross-and-triangle-spread/

11 Popular Tarot Spreads for Beginners and Advanced readers. (2022, January 21). A Little Spark of Joy. https://www.alittlesparkofjoy.com/easy-tarot-spreads/

Esselmont, B. (n.d.). 9 Sure-Fire Ways to Select a Tarot Deck That's Right for You. Biddy Tarot. https://www.biddytarot.com/selecting-a-tarot-deck/

Examining Relationships with Tarot - 3 Love Tarot Spreads to Understand You & Your Partner. (2017, February 25). Labyrinthos. https://labyrinthos.co/blogs/learn-tarot-with-labyrinthos-academy/examining-relationships-with-tarot-3-love-tarot-spreads-to-understand-you-your-partner

Learning & Using the Zodiac Tarot Spread. (n.d.). The Simple Tarot. https://thesimpletarot.com/learning-using-zodiac-tarot-spread/

Major Arcana Tarot Card Meanings. (n.d.). Biddy Tarot. https://www.biddytarot.com/tarot-card-meanings/major-arcana/

May, A. (n.d.). Crystal Correspondences – The Most Comprehensive Guide Ever. Wicca Now. https://wiccanow.com/crystal-correspondences/

Minor Arcana Tarot Card Meanings. (n.d.). Biddy Tarot. https://www.biddytarot.com/tarot-card-meanings/minor-arcana/

Oldale, R. J. (2020, July 15). What Do The Four Elements Represent In People? Master Mind Content. https://www.mastermindcontent.co.uk/what-do-the-four-elements-represent-in-people/

Parlett, D. (2009, April 7). tarot. Encyclopedia Britannica. https://www.britannica.com/topic/tarot

Pentagram Tarot Spread. (2021, January 19). Northern Lights Wicca. https://northernlightswicca.com/2021/01/19/pentagram-tarot-spread/

Regan, S. (2021, September 15). 10 Easy Ways To Cleanse Your Tarot Cards & Why You Need To. mindbodygreen. https://www.mindbodygreen.com/articles/how-to-cleanse-tarot-cards

Russell, D. (n.d.). 3-Card Tarot Spreads: 25 Simple Layouts For Insight & Inspiration. Davy & Tracy. https://davyandtracy.com/tarot/3-card-tarot-spreads/

Tarot Card Meanings List. (n.d.). Labyrinthos. https://labyrinthos.co/blogs/tarot-card-meanings-list

References

Timmons, J. (2022, February 22). How To Do A Basic Tarot Reading For Yourself Or A Friend. Mindbodygreen. https://www.mindbodygreen.com/0-18172/how-to-do-a-basic-tarot-reading-for-yourself-or-a-friend.html

Tracey, J. (n.d.). Horoscope Tarot Spread with Jo Tracey. Biddy Tarot. https://www.biddytarot.com/horoscope-tarot-spread-jo-tracey/

Wigington, P. (2019, January 5). Seven Card Horseshoe Tarot Spread. Learn Religions. https://www.learnreligions.com/seven-card-horseshoe-tarot-spread-2562801

Wigington, P. (2019, March 11). The Romany Spread Tarot Card Layout. Learn Religions. https://www.learnreligions.com/romany-spread-tarot-cards-4588969

Yotka, S. (2016, August 4). Tarot 101: A Beginner's Guide. Vogue. https://www.vogue.com/article/tarot-101-beginner-guide-how-to-small-spells

About the Author

Monique Joiner Siedlak is a writer, witch, and warrior on a mission to awaken people to their greatest potential through the power of storytelling infused with mysticism, modern paganism, and new age spirituality. At the young age of 12, she began rigorously studying the fascinating philosophy of Wicca. By the time she was 20, she was self-initiated into the craft, and hasn't looked back ever since. To this day, she has authored over 40 books pertaining to the magick and mysteries of life.

To find out more about Monique Joiner Siedlak artistically, spiritually, and personally, feel free to visit her **official website**.

www.mojosiedlak.com

facebook.com/mojosiedlak
twitter.com/mojosiedlak
instagram.com/mojosiedlak
pinterest.com/mojosiedlak
youtube.com/@MoniqueJoinerSiedlak_Author
bookbub.com/authors/monique-joiner-siedlak

More Books by Monique

African Spirituality Beliefs and Practices

Hoodoo

Seven African Powers: The Orishas

Cooking for the Orishas

Lucumi: The Ways of Santeria

Voodoo of Louisiana

Haitian Vodou

Orishas of Trinidad

Connecting With Your Ancestors

Black Magic

The Orishas

Vodun: West Africa's Spiritual Life

Marie Laveau: Life of a Voodoo Queen

More Books by Monique

Candomblé: Dancing for the Gods

Practical Magick

Wiccan Basics

Candle Magick

Wiccan Spells

Love Spells

Abundance Spells

Herb Magick

Moon Magick

Creating Your Own Spells

Gypsy Magic

Protection Magick

Celtic Magick

Shamanic Magick

Crystal Magick

Personal and Self Development

Creative Visualization

Astral Projection for Beginners

Meditation for Beginners

Reiki for Beginners

Manifesting With the Law of Attraction

Stress Management

Being an Empath Today

More Books by Monique

Life on Fire

Healing Your Inner Child: A Guide into Shadow Work

Change Your Life: How to Use the Universal Laws of Nature to Manifest Your Desires

Raising Your Vibe: The Guide for Becoming a Lightworker

Get a Handle on Life

Get a Handle on Anxiety

Get a Handle on Depression

Get a Handle on Procrastination

The Yoga Collective

Yoga for Beginners

Yoga for Stress

Yoga for Back Pain

Yoga for Weight Loss

Yoga for Flexibility

Yoga for Advanced Beginners

Yoga for Fitness

Yoga for Runners

Yoga for Energy

Yoga for Your Sex Life

Yoga to Beat Depression and Anxiety

Yoga for Menstruation

Yoga to Detox Your Body

More Books by Monique

Yoga to Tone Your Body

A Natural Beautiful You

Creating Your Own Body Butter

Creating Your Own Body Scrub

Creating Your Own Body Spray

www.ingramcontent.com/pod-product-compliance
Lightning Source LLC
Chambersburg PA
CBHW060833050426
42453CB00008B/681